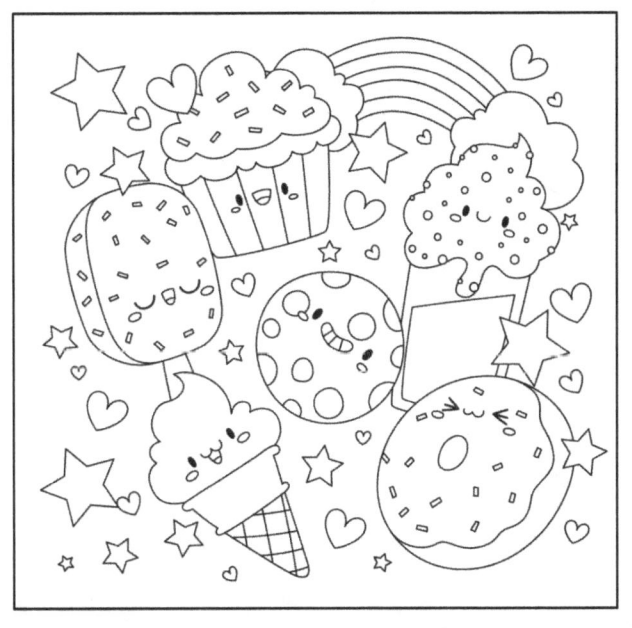

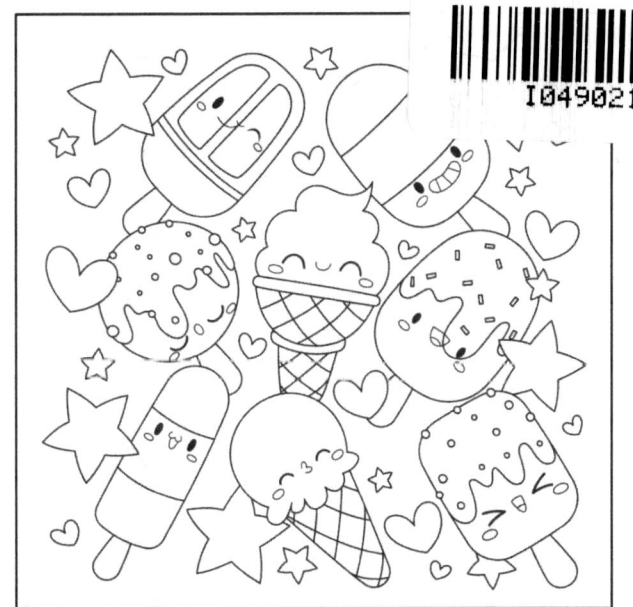

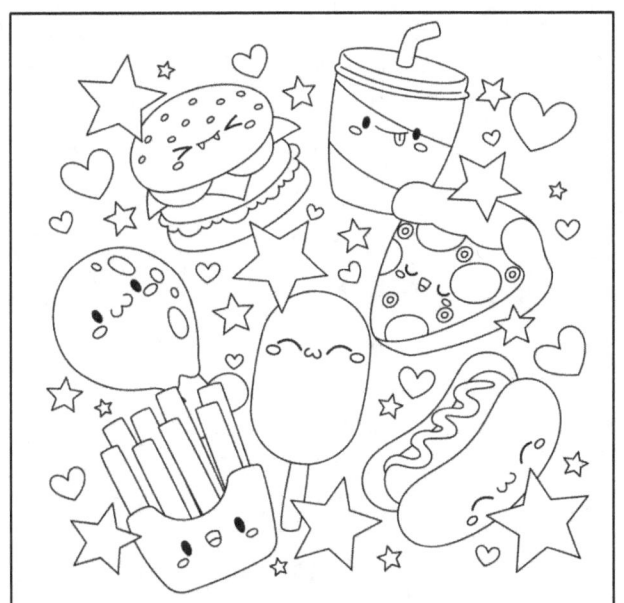

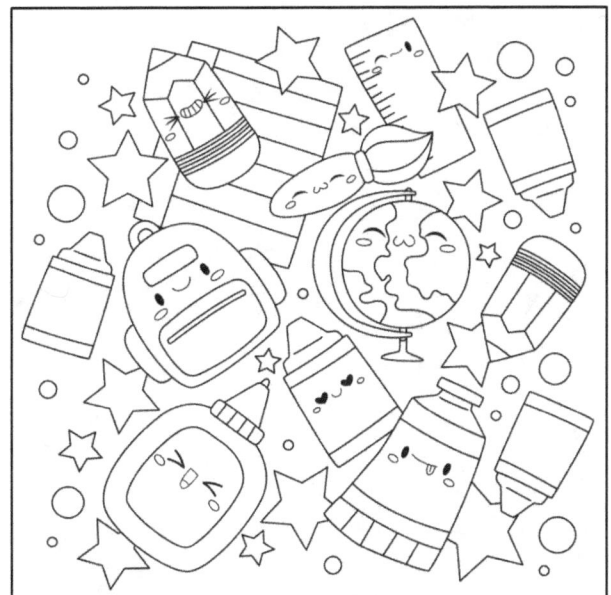

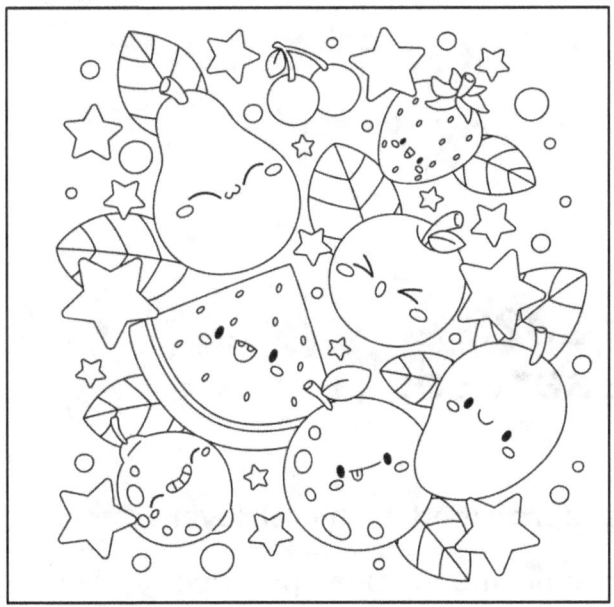

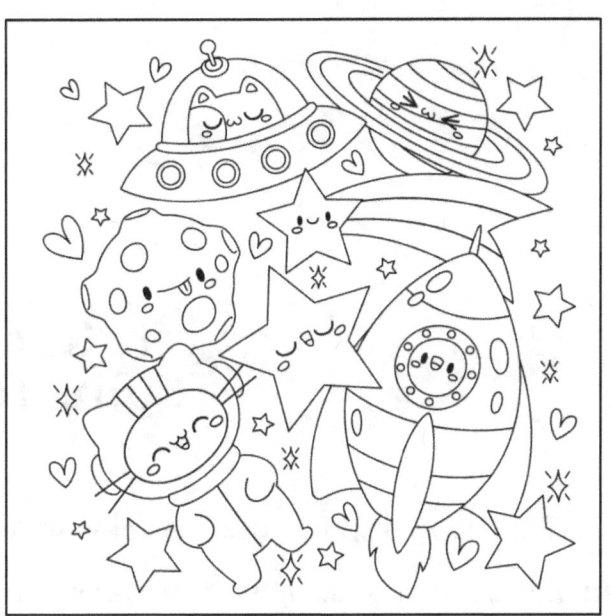

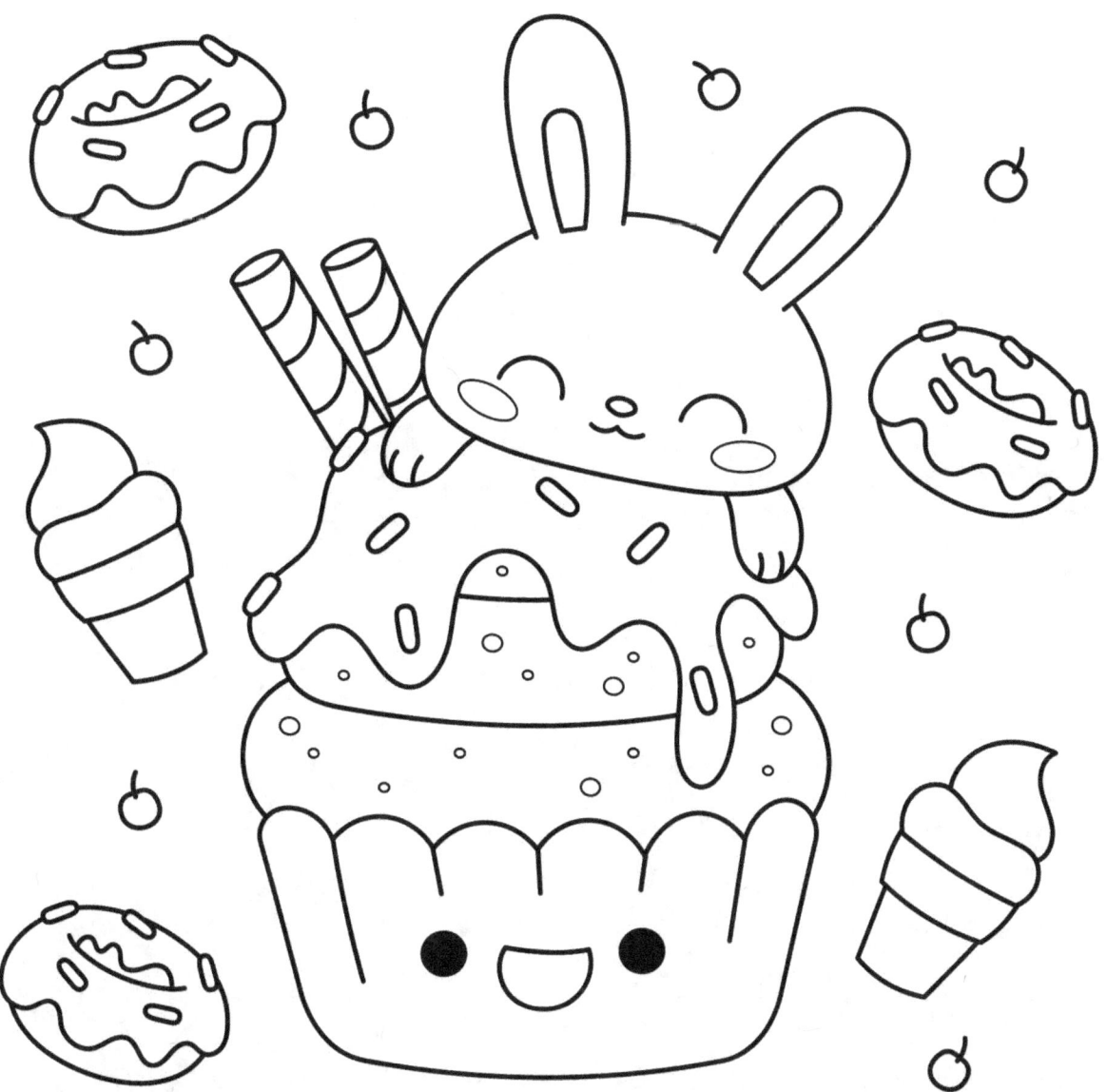

THIS BOOK BELONGS TO

_____

CUTE KAWAII
Coloring Book

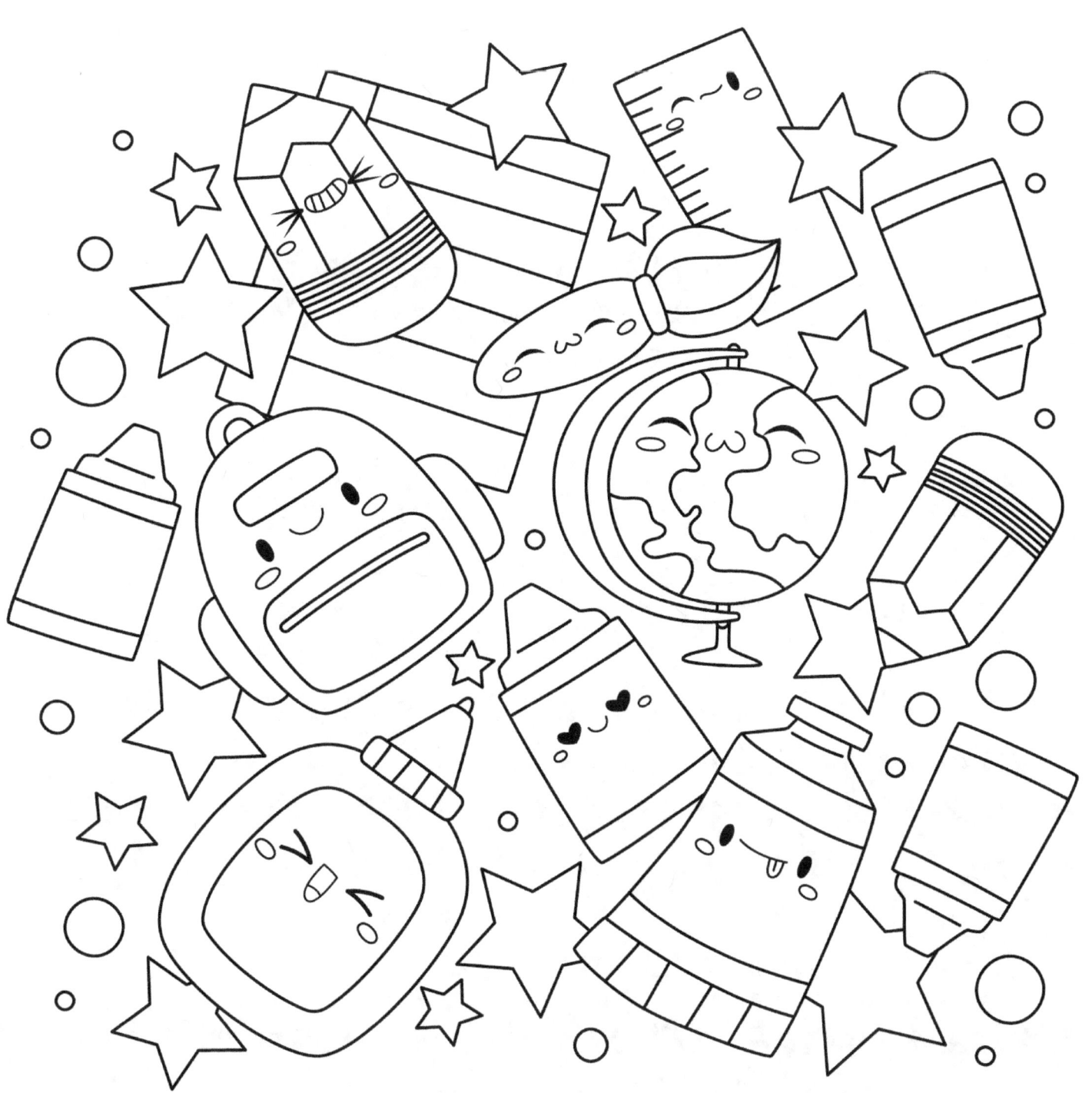

CUTE KAWAII
Coloring Book

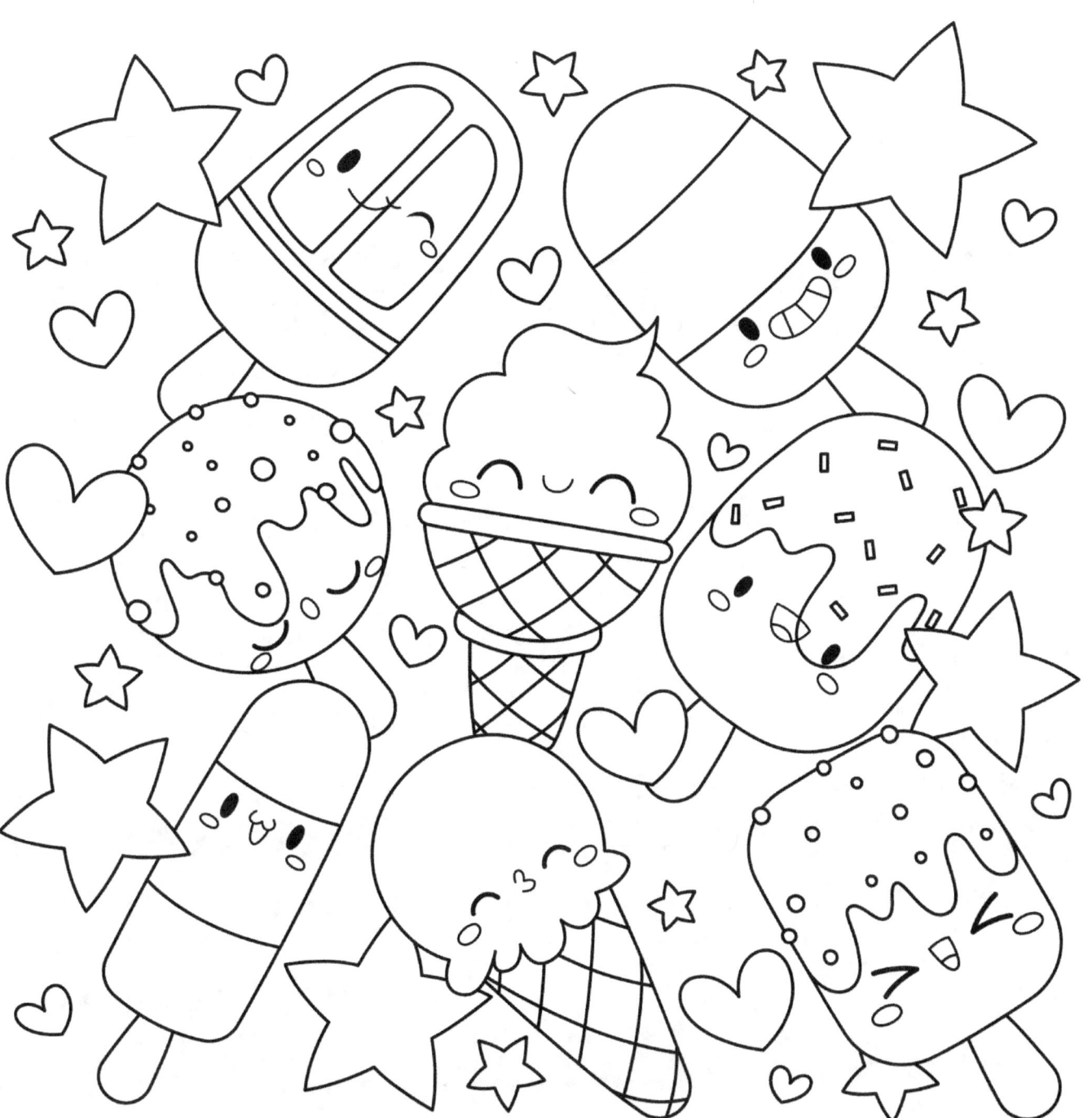

CUTE KAWAII
Coloring Book

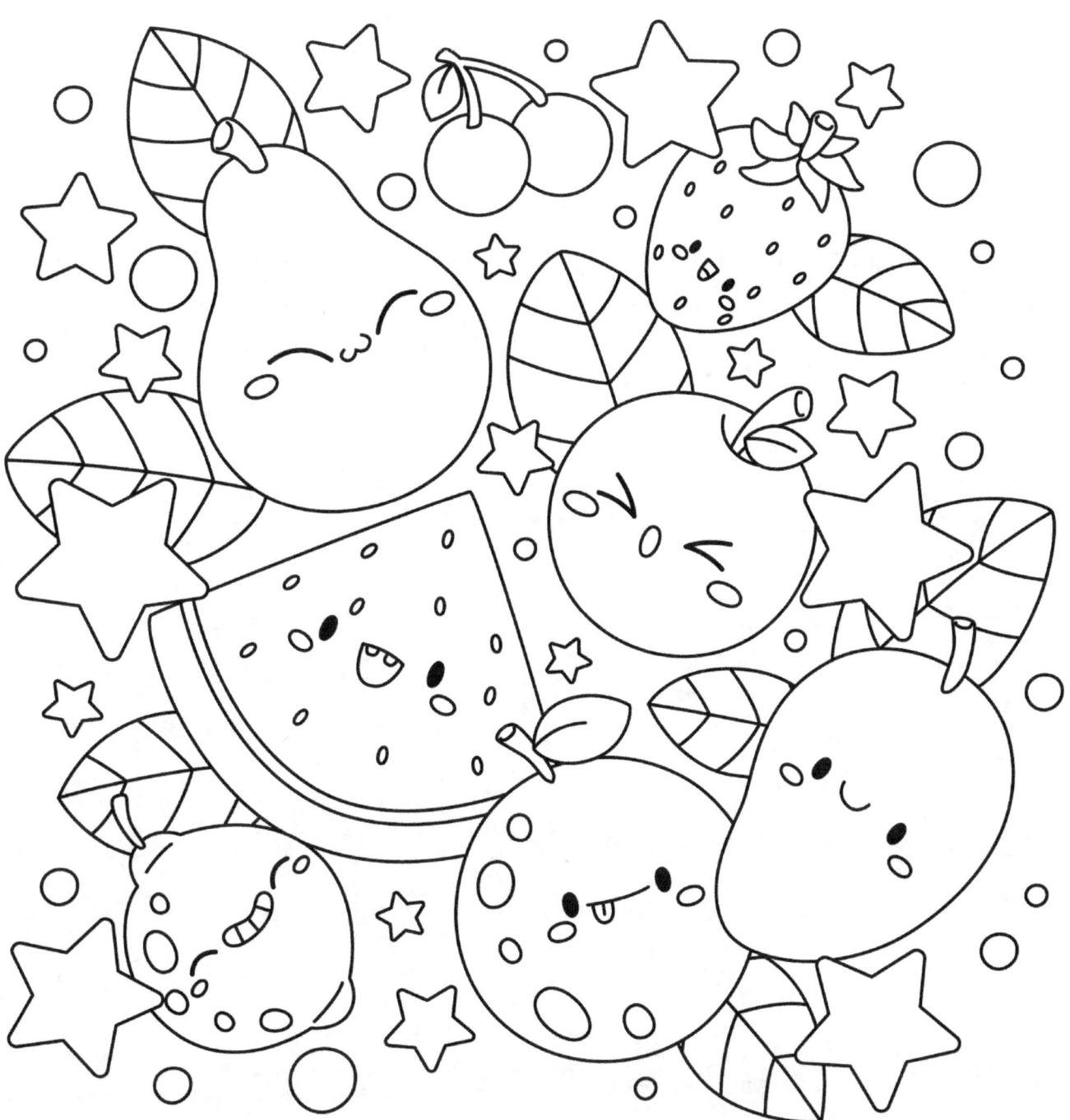

CUTE KAWAII
Coloring Book

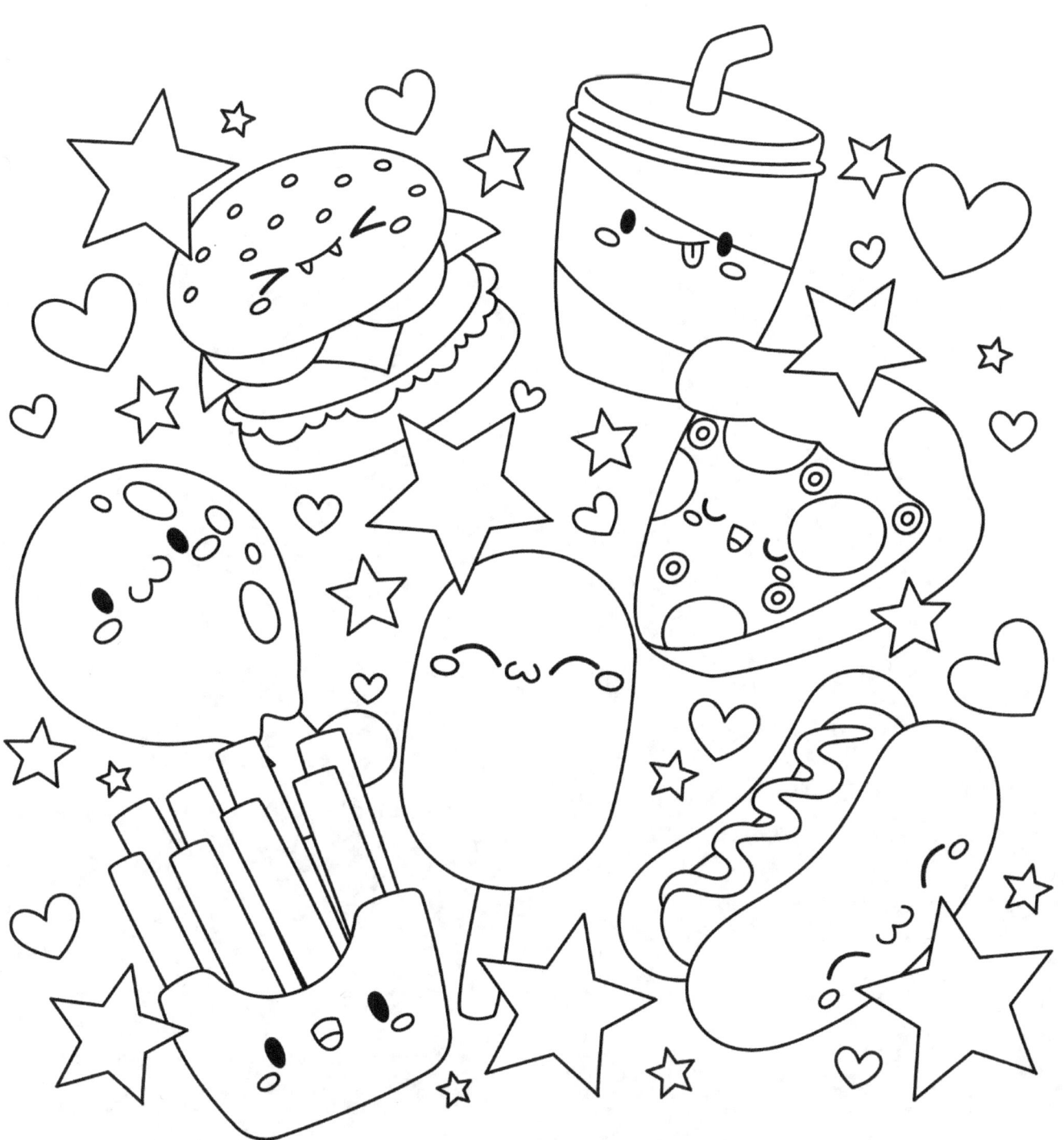

CUTE KAWAII
Coloring Book

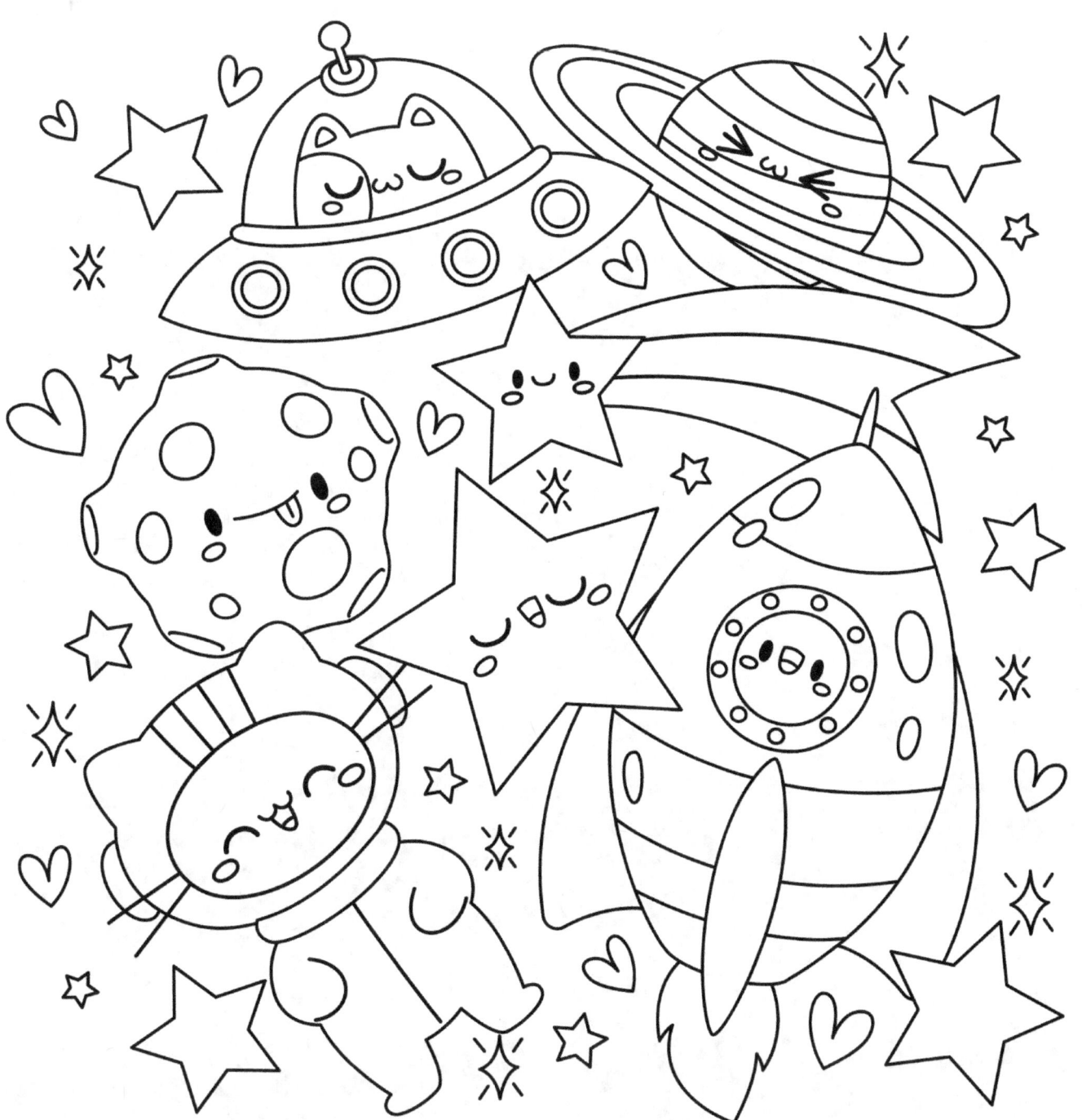

CUTE KAWAII
Coloring Book

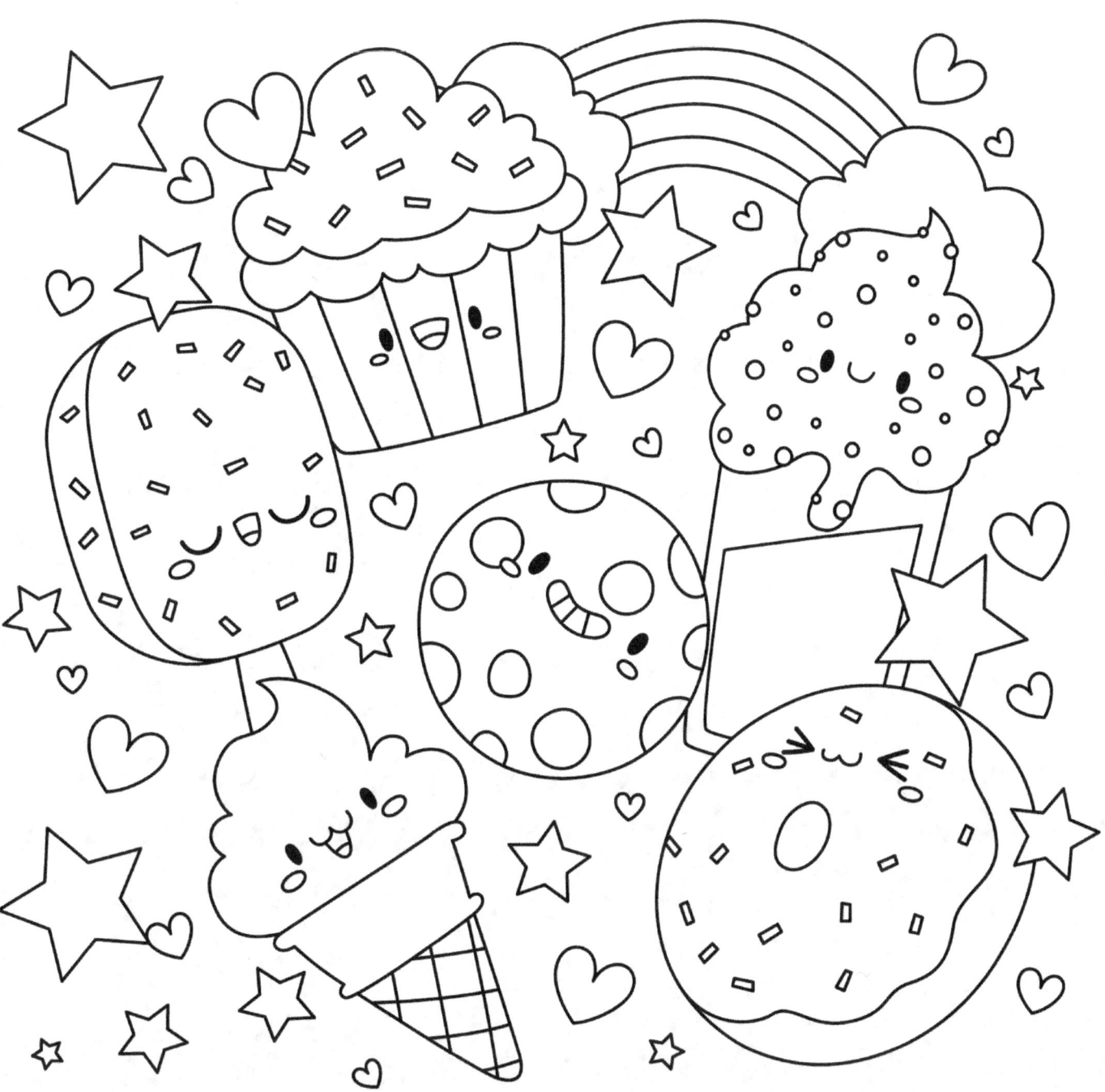

CUTE KAWAII
Coloring Book

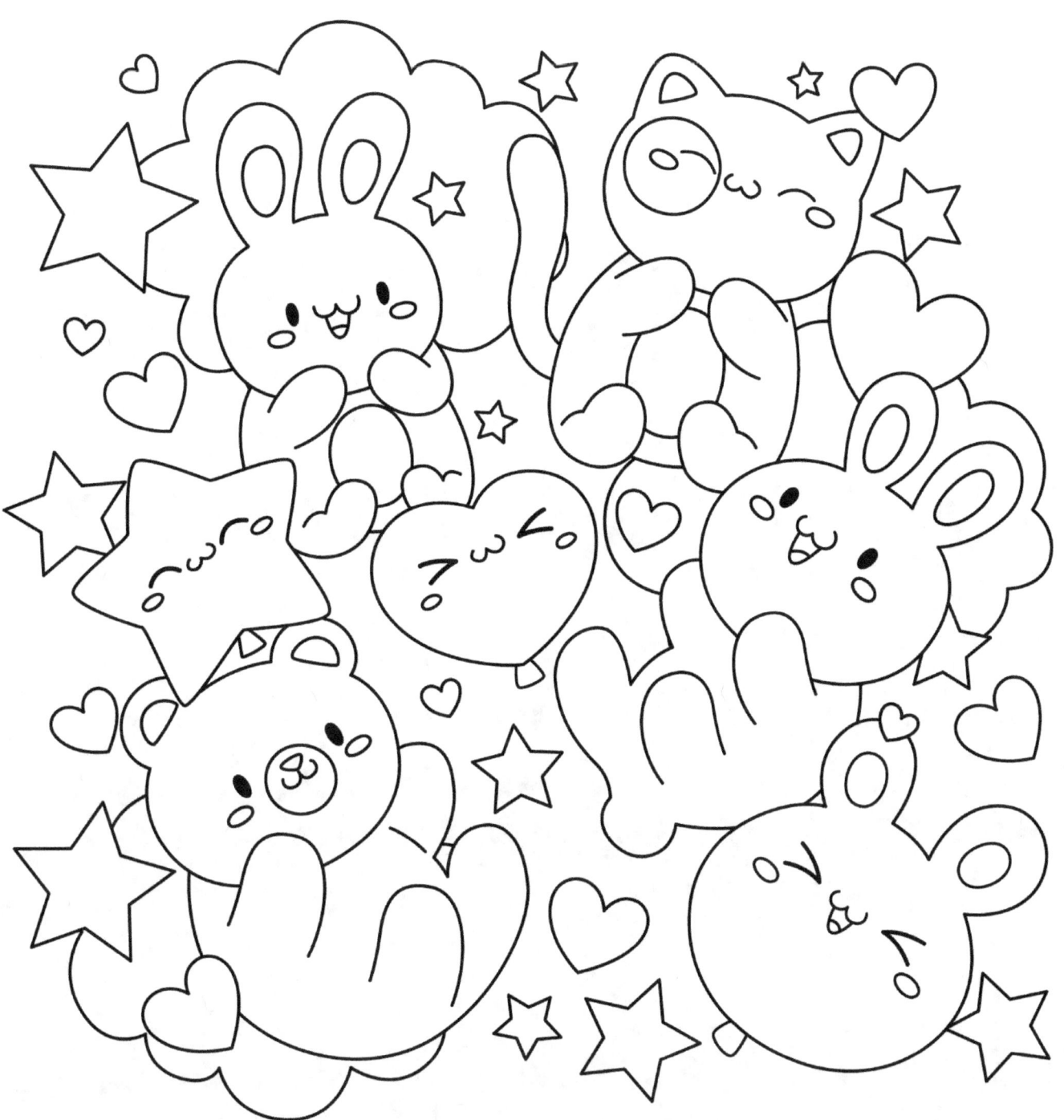

CUTE KAWAII
Coloring Book

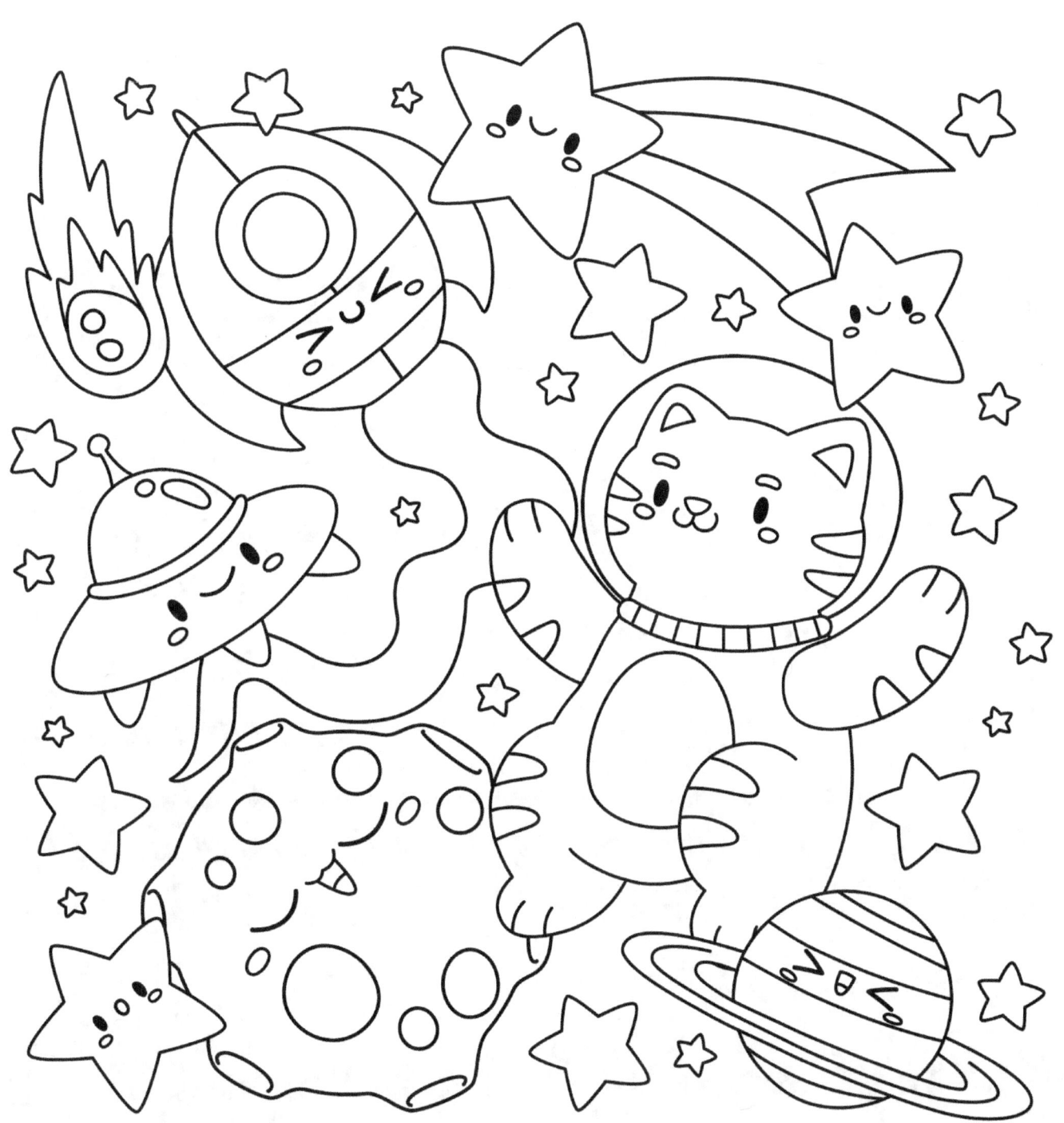

CUTE KAWAII
Coloring Book

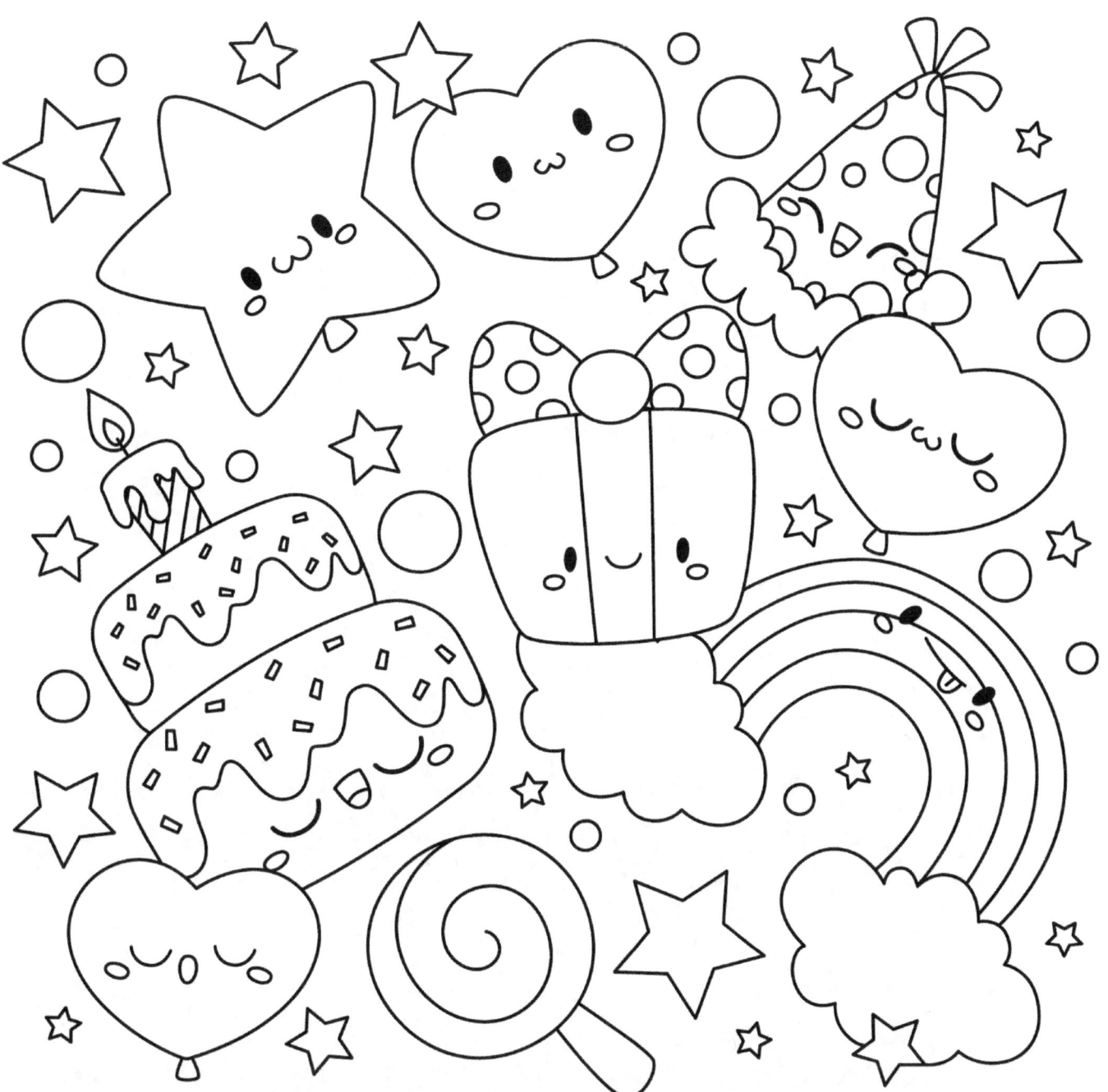

CUTE KAWAII
Coloring Book

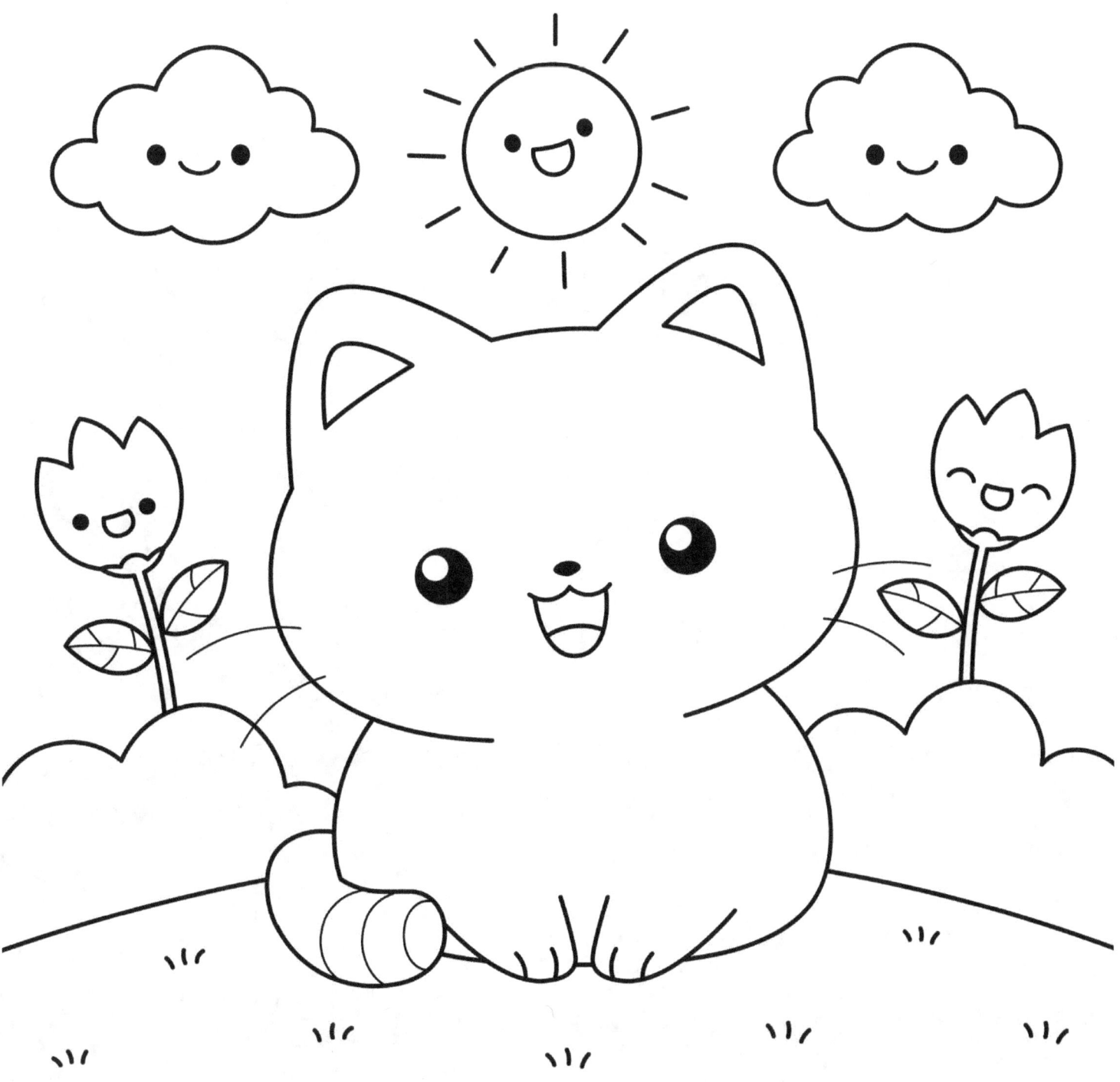

CUTE KAWAII
Coloring Book

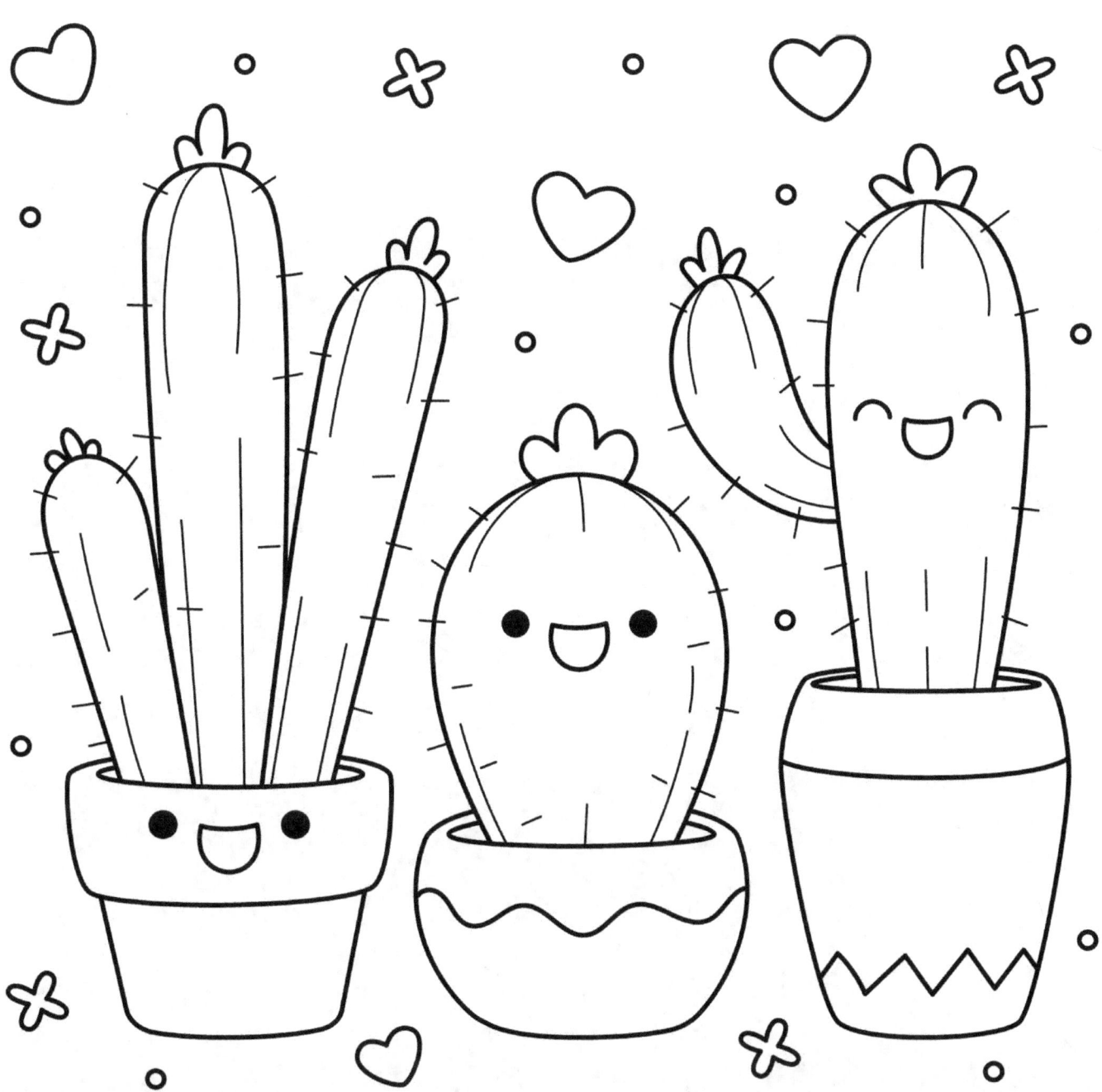

CUTE KAWAII
Coloring Book

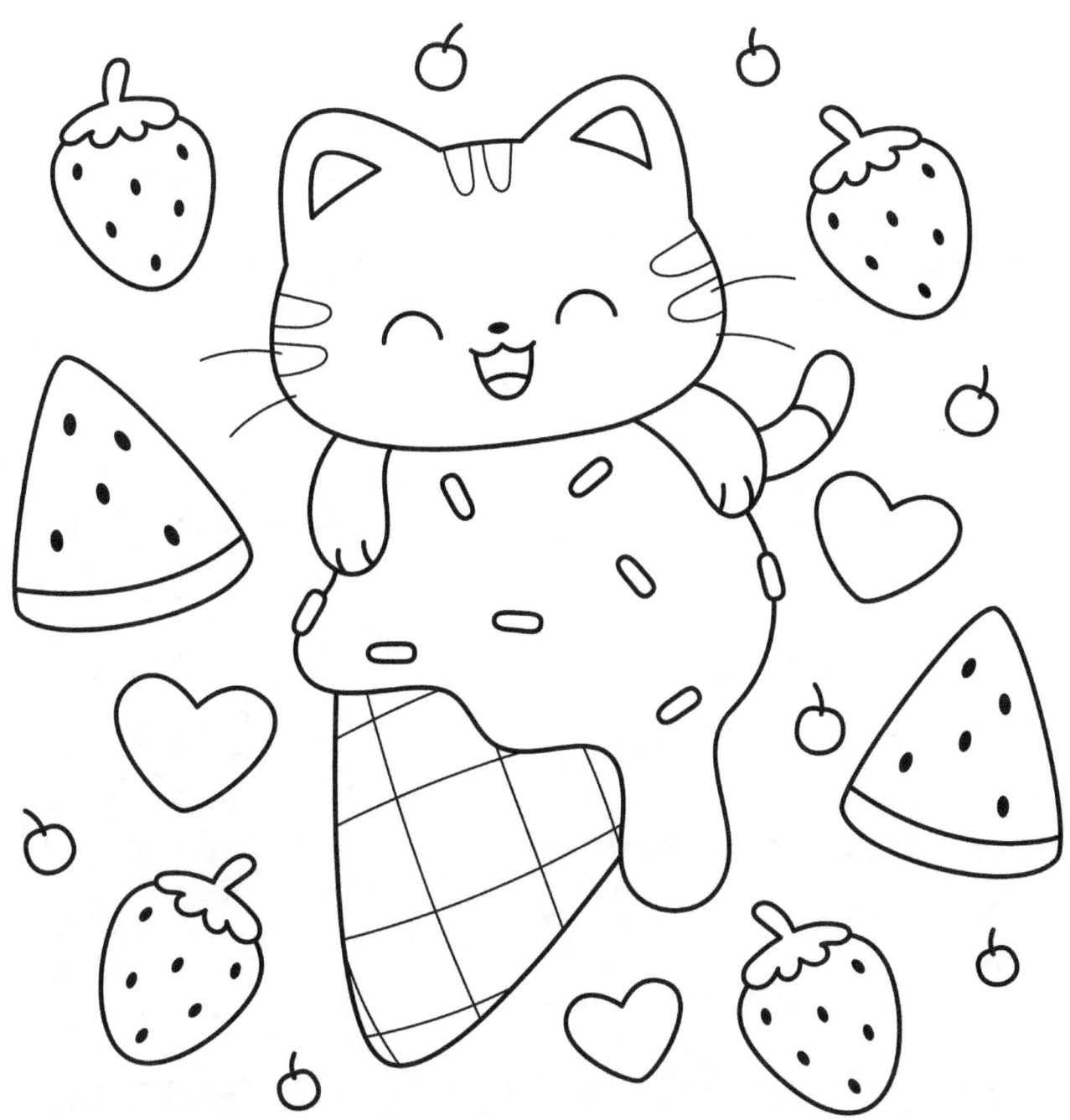

CUTE KAWAII
Coloring Book

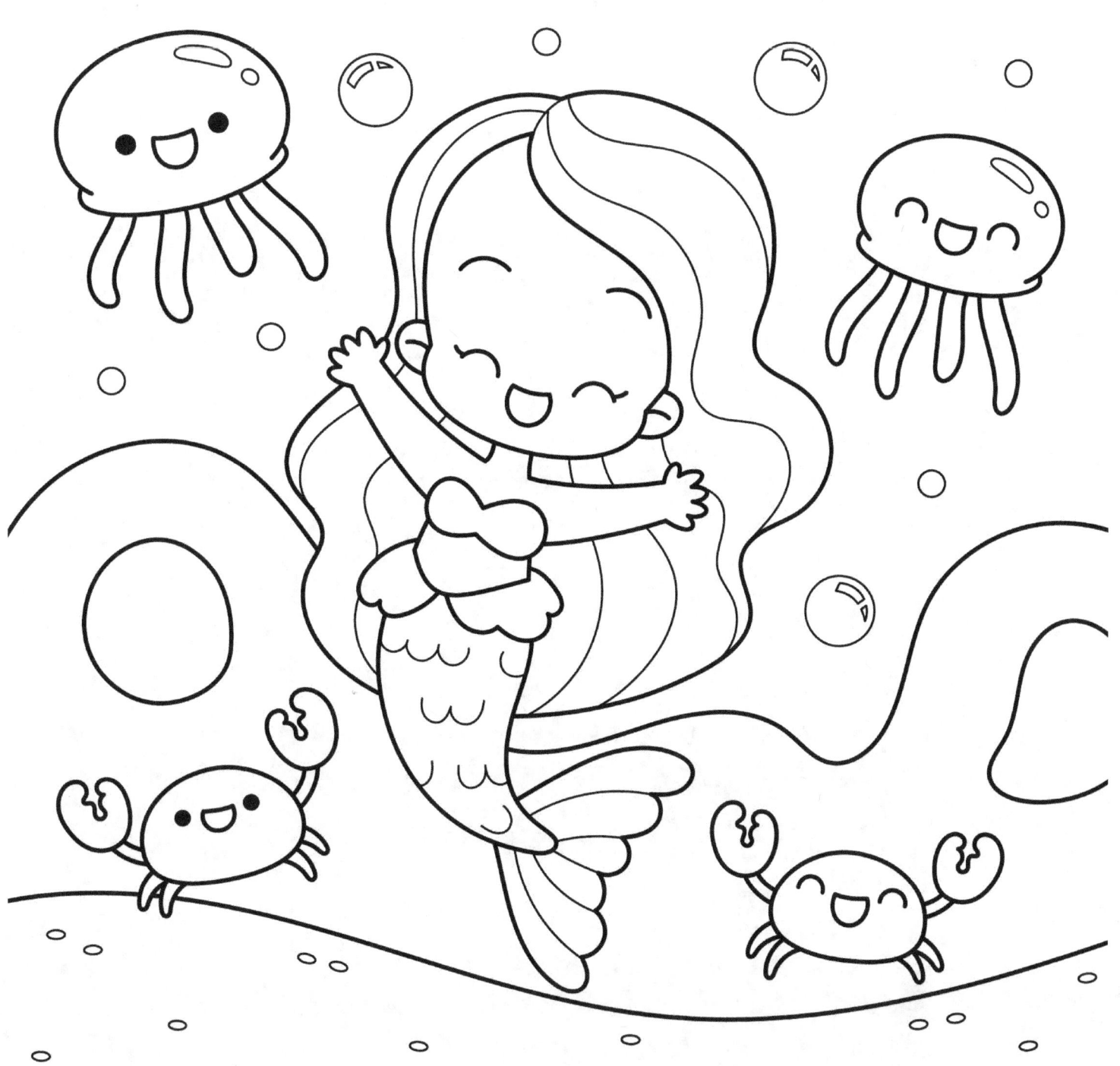

CUTE KAWAII
Coloring Book

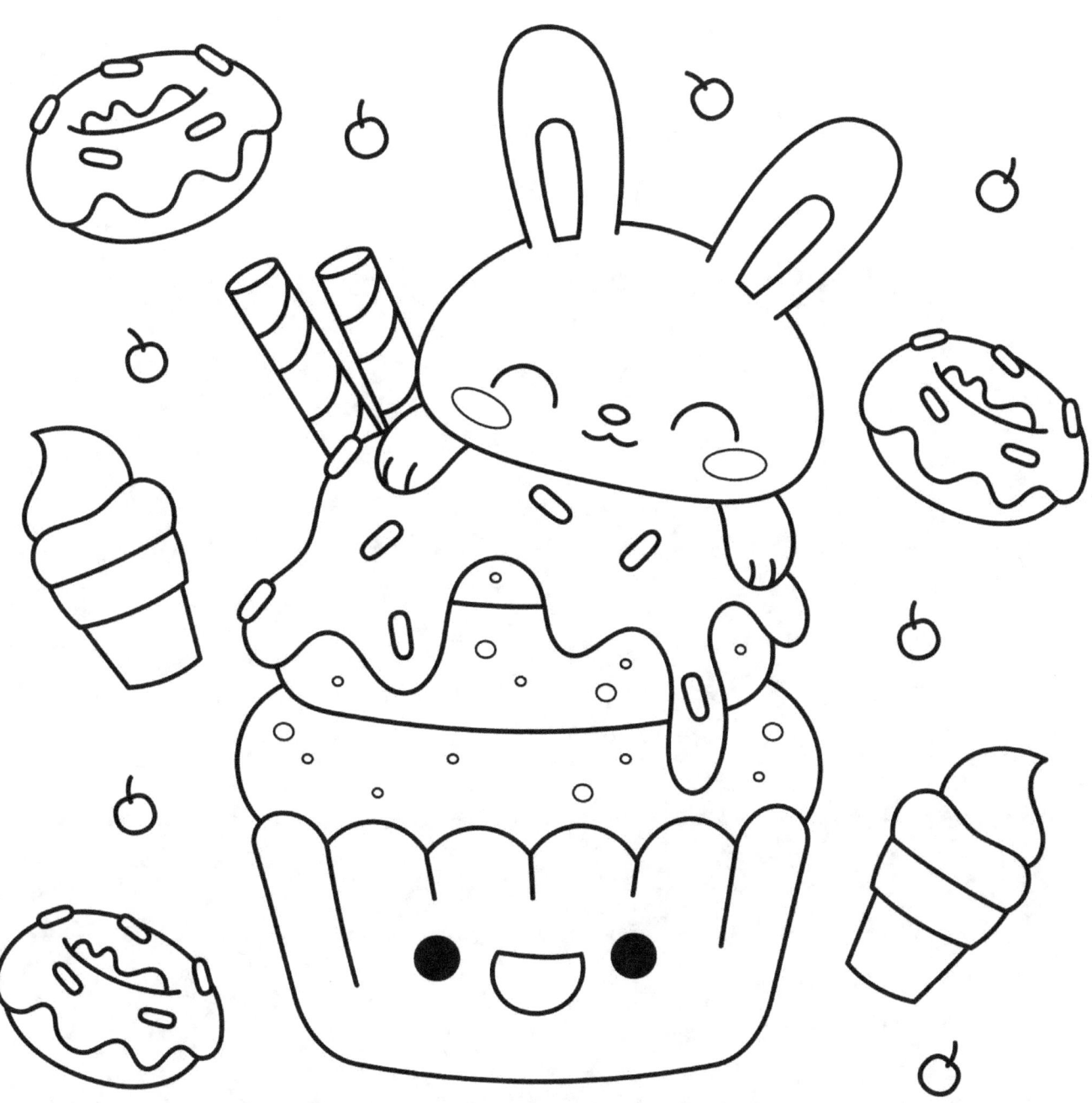

CUTE KAWAII
Coloring Book

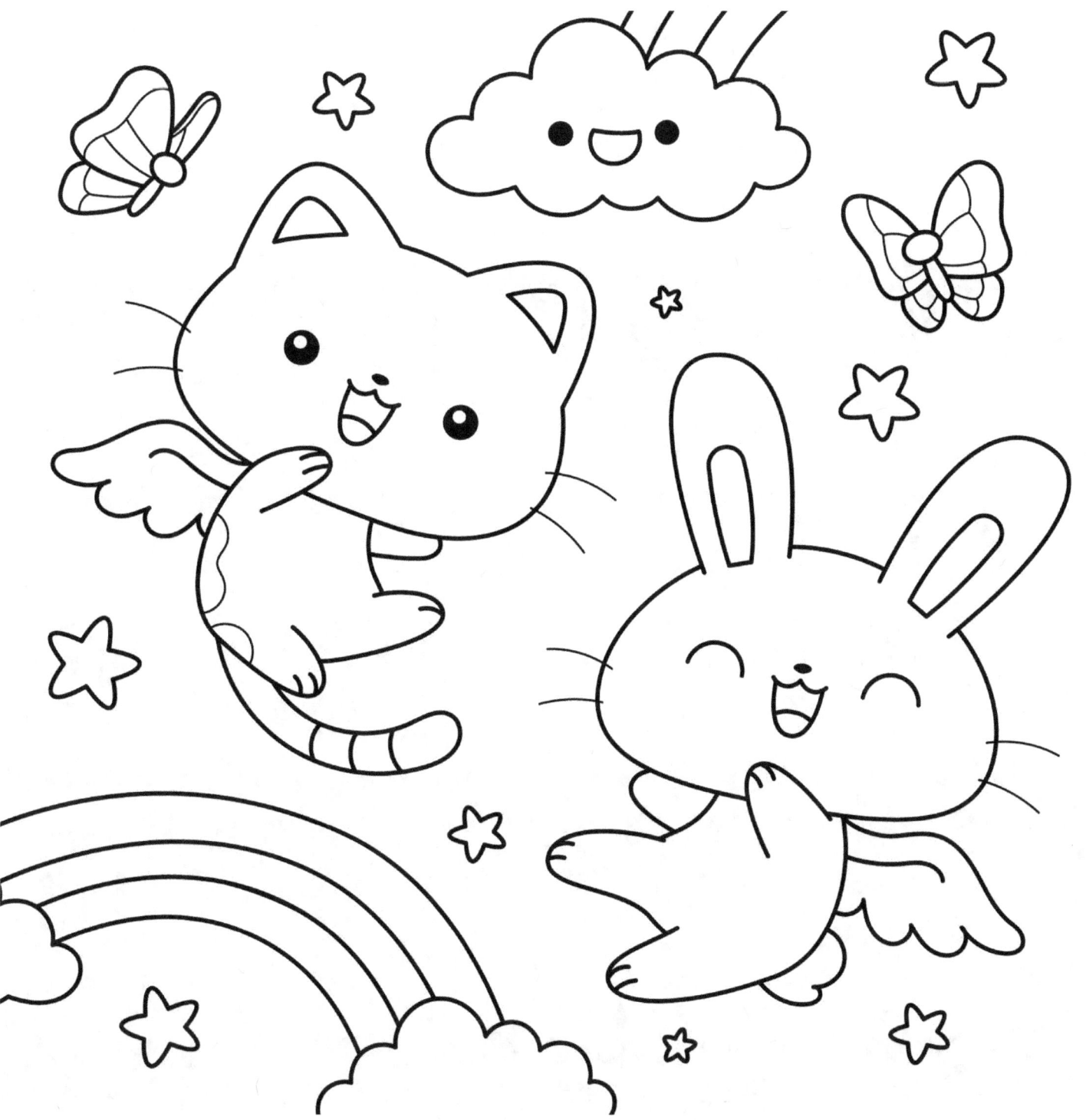

CUTE KAWAII
Coloring Book

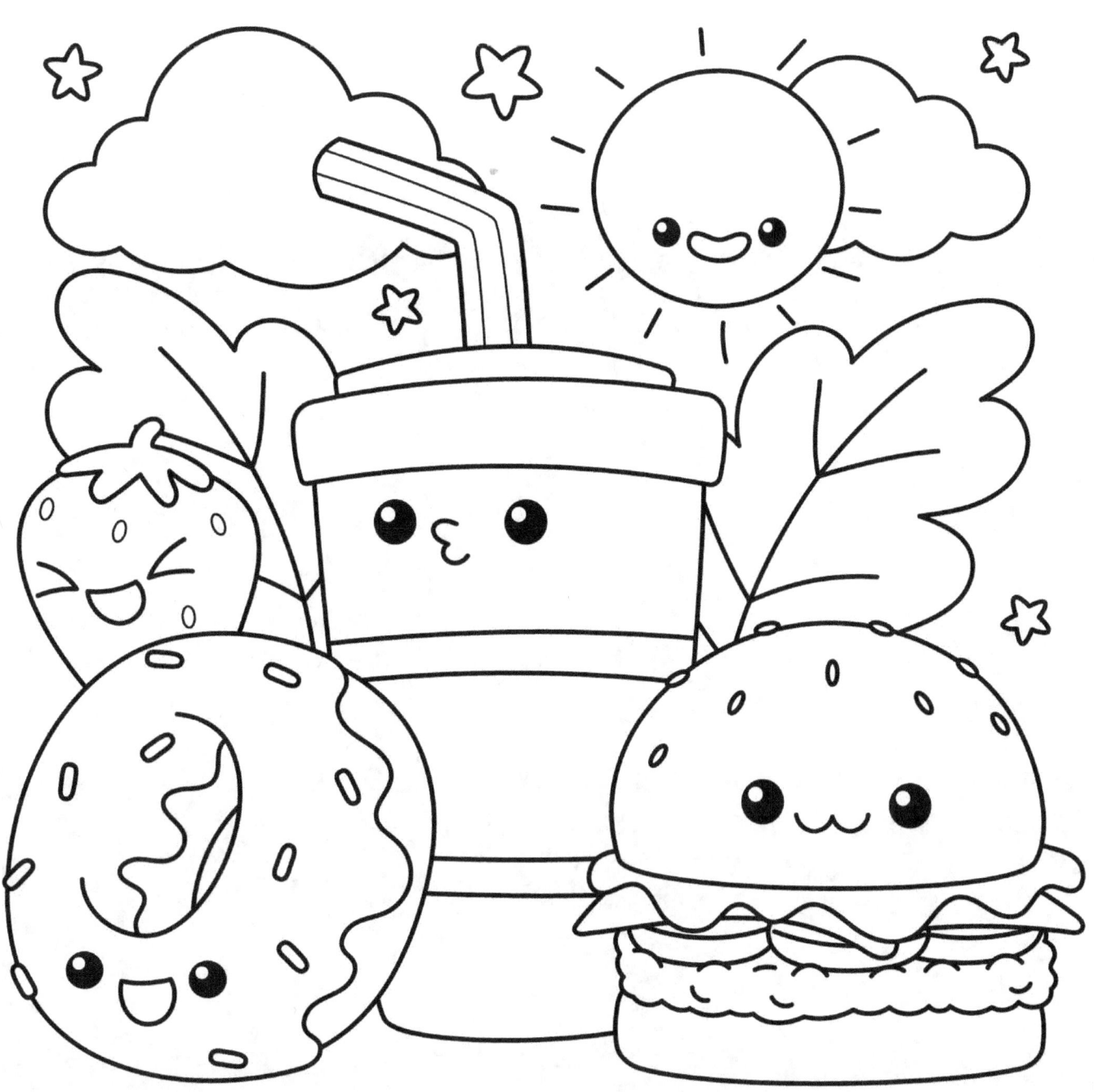

CUTE KAWAII
Coloring Book

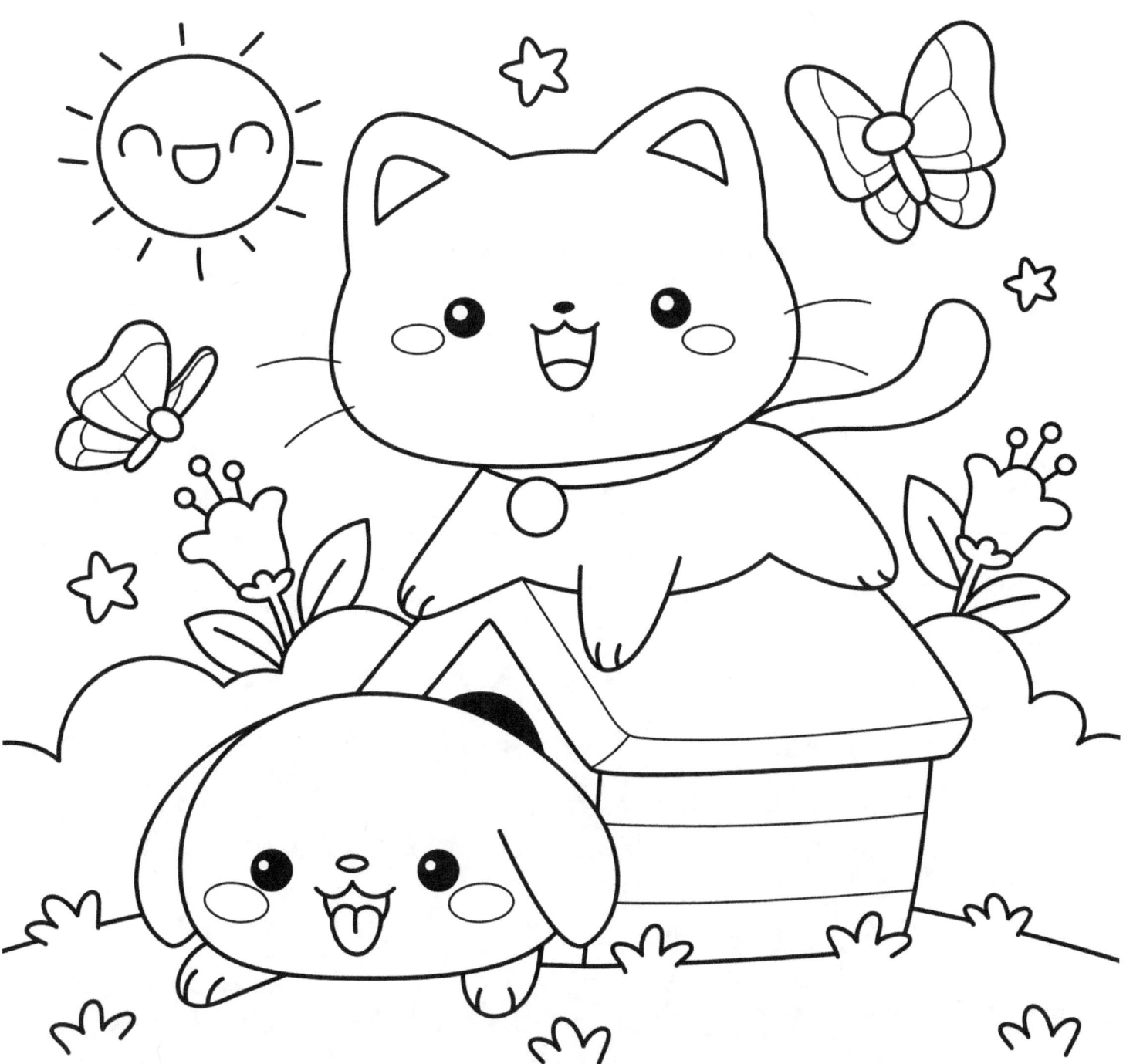

CUTE KAWAII
Coloring Book

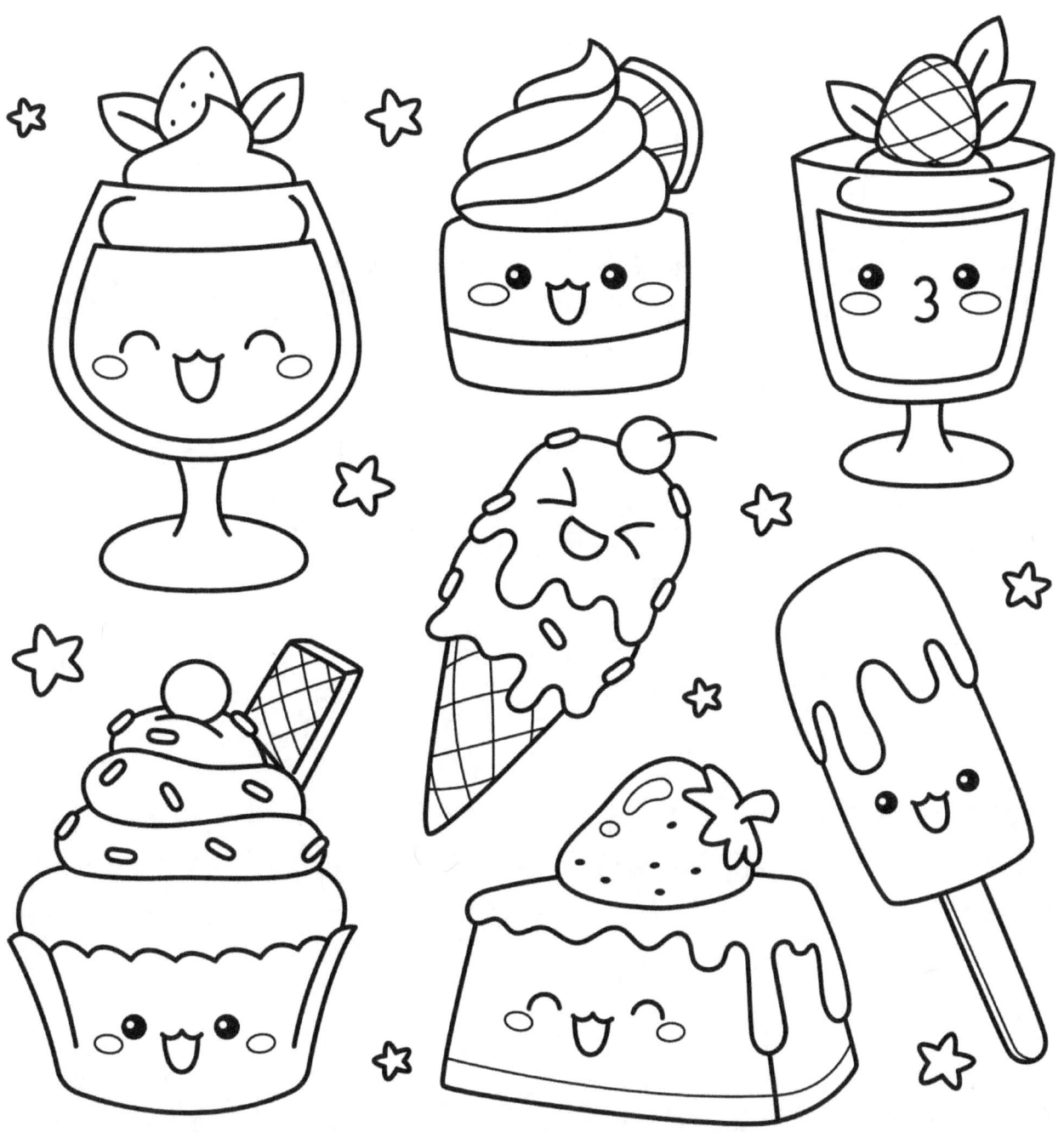

CUTE KAWAII
Coloring Book

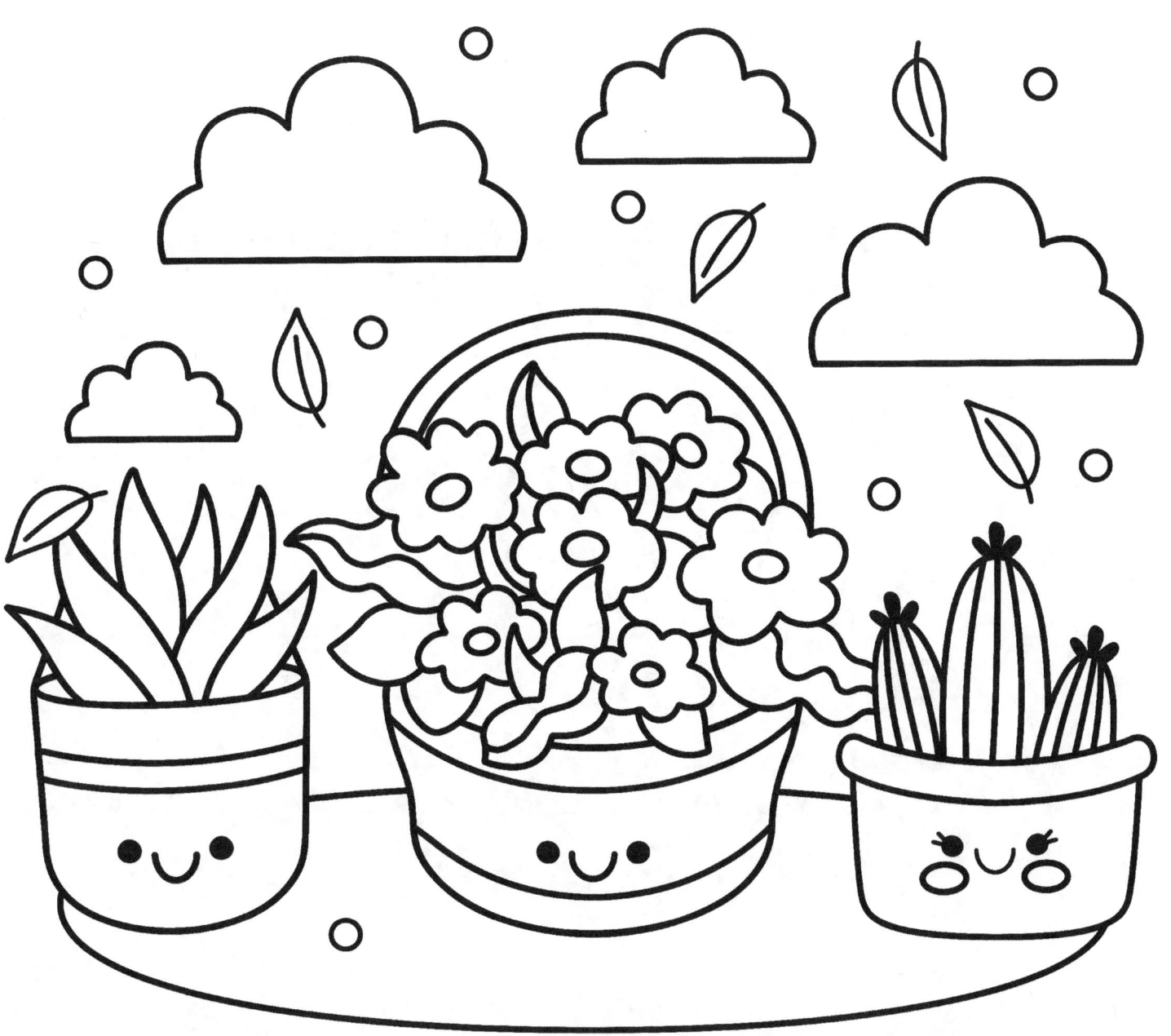

CUTE KAWAII
Coloring Book

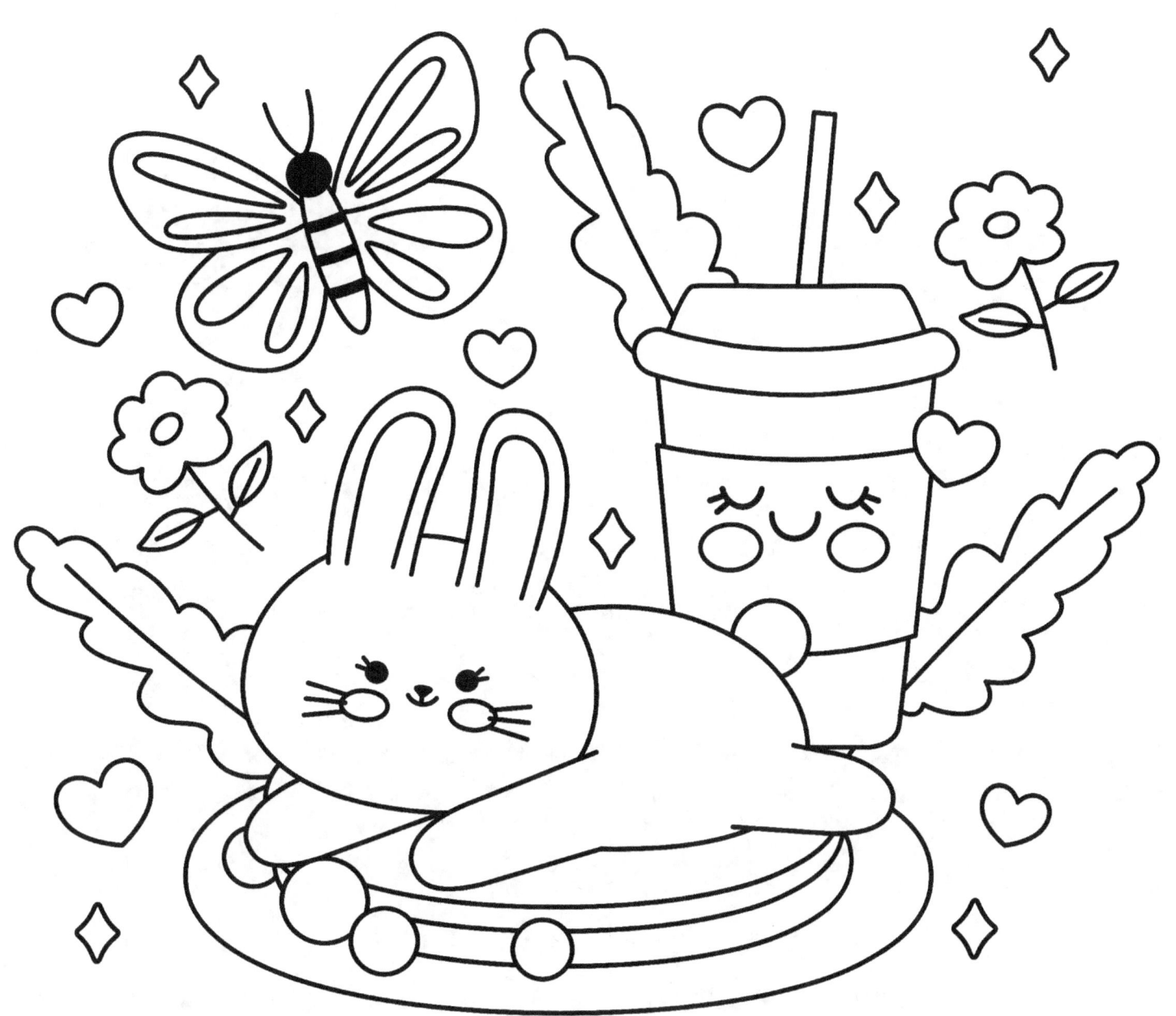

CUTE KAWAII

Coloring Book

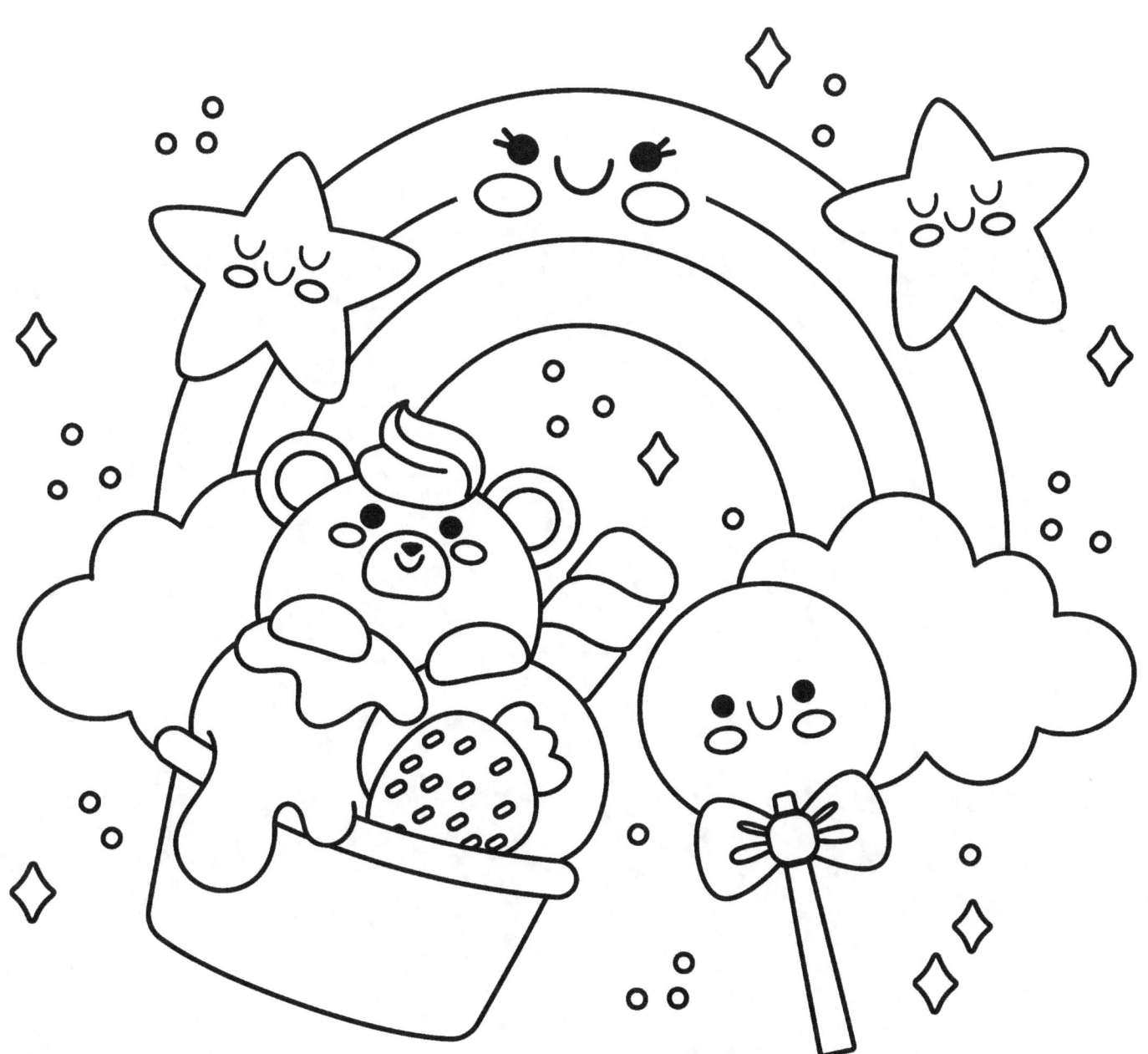

CUTE KAWAII
Coloring Book

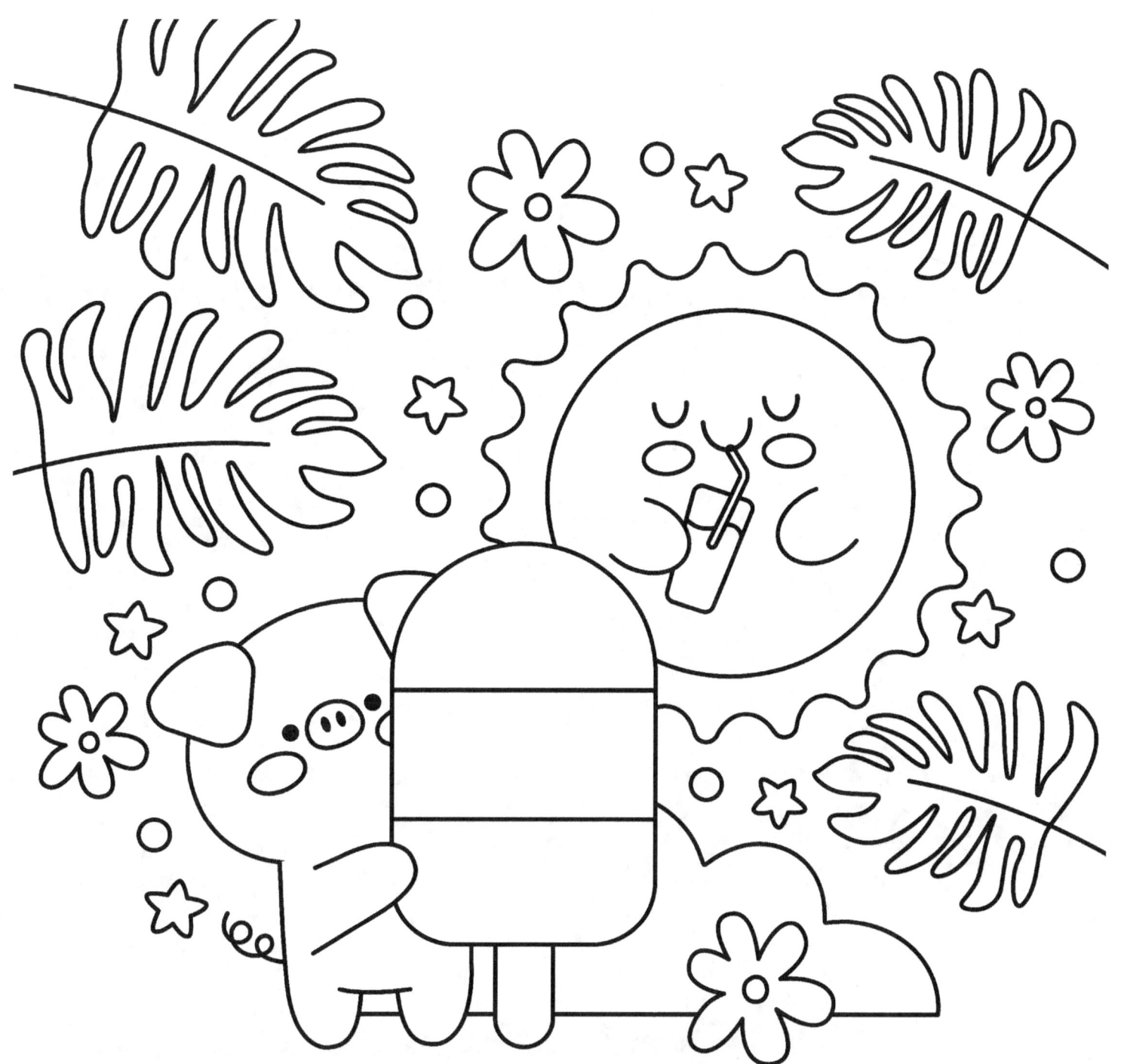

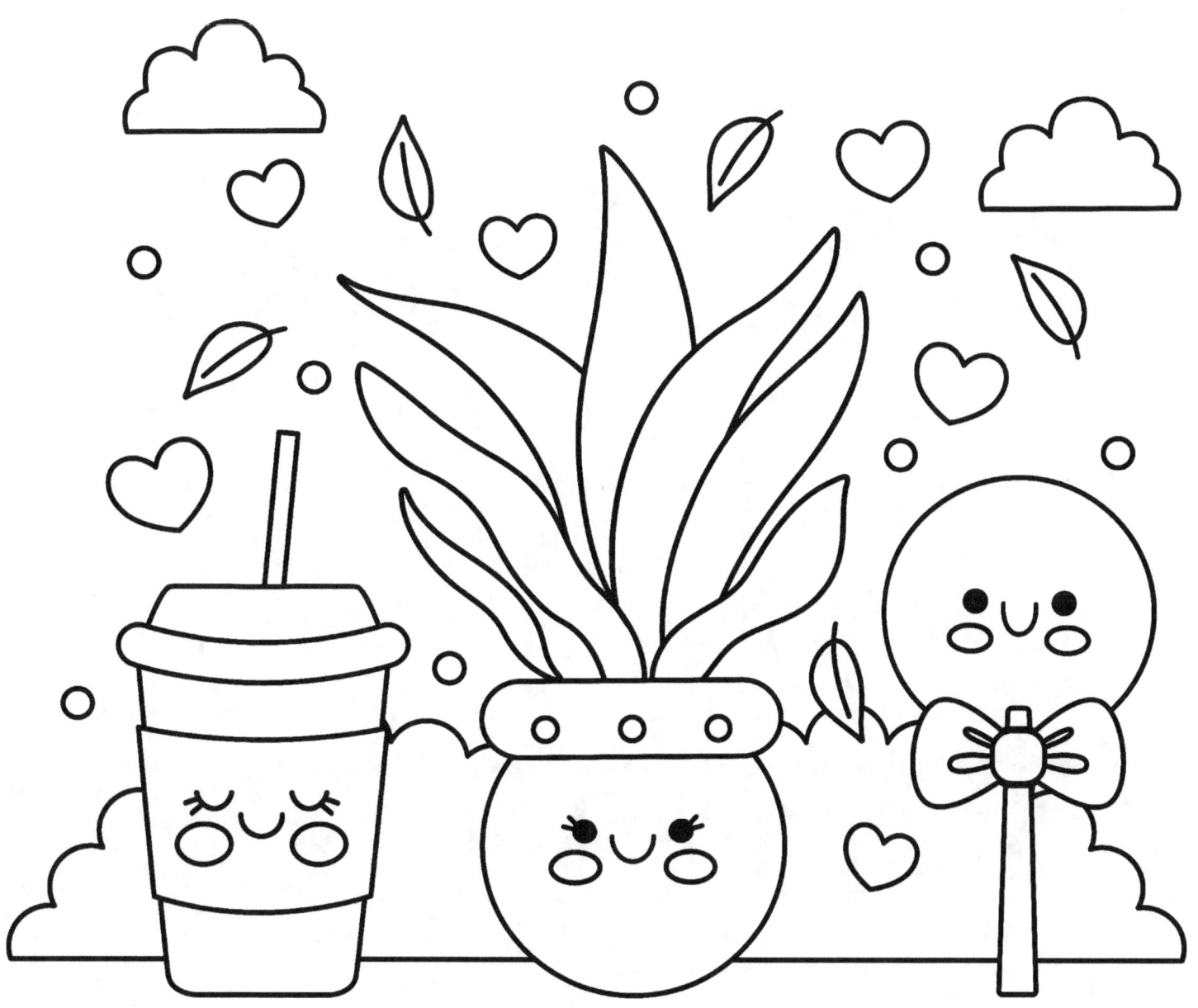

CUTE KAWAII
Coloring Book

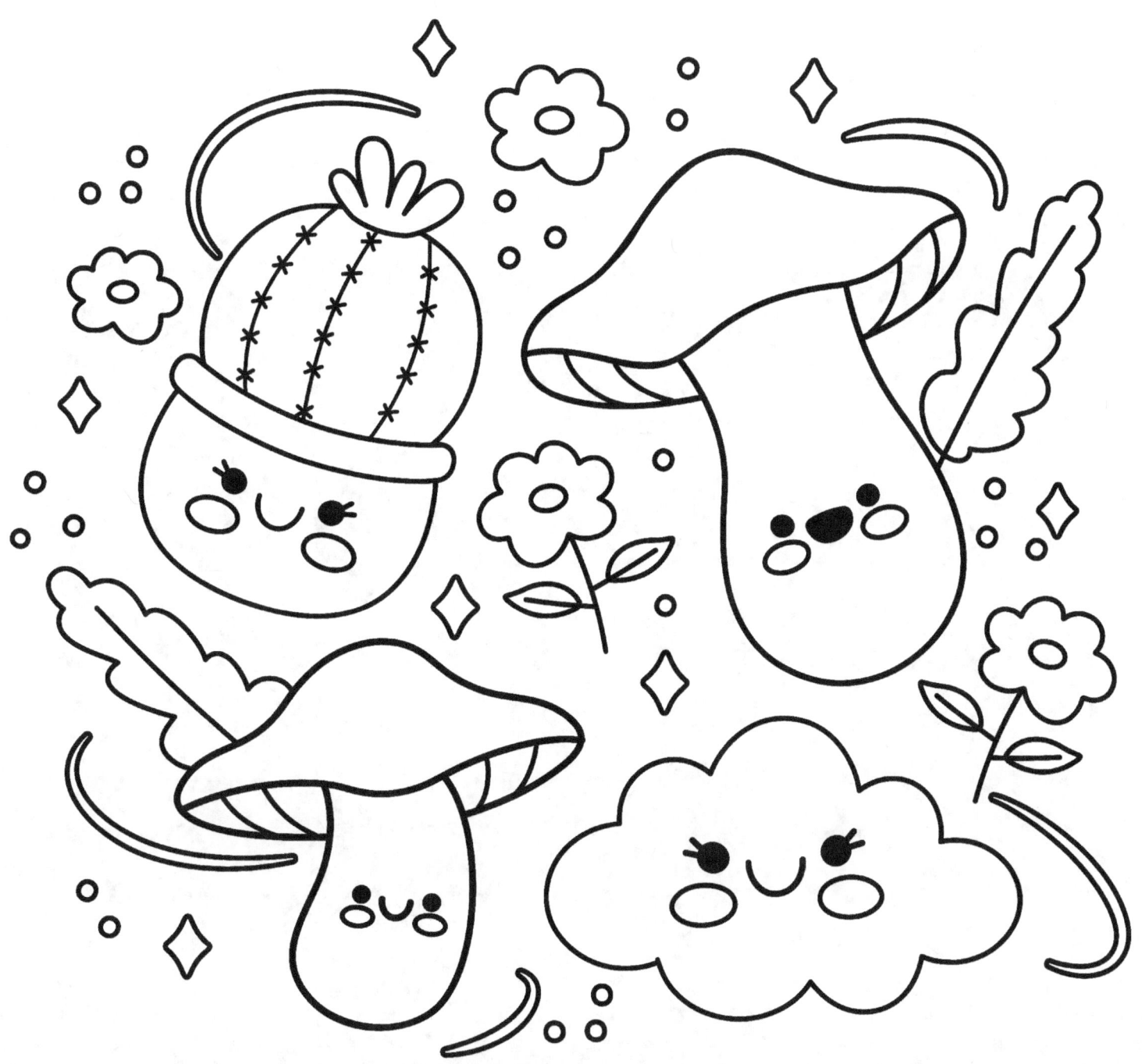

CUTE KAWAII

Coloring Book

CUTE KAWAII
Coloring Book

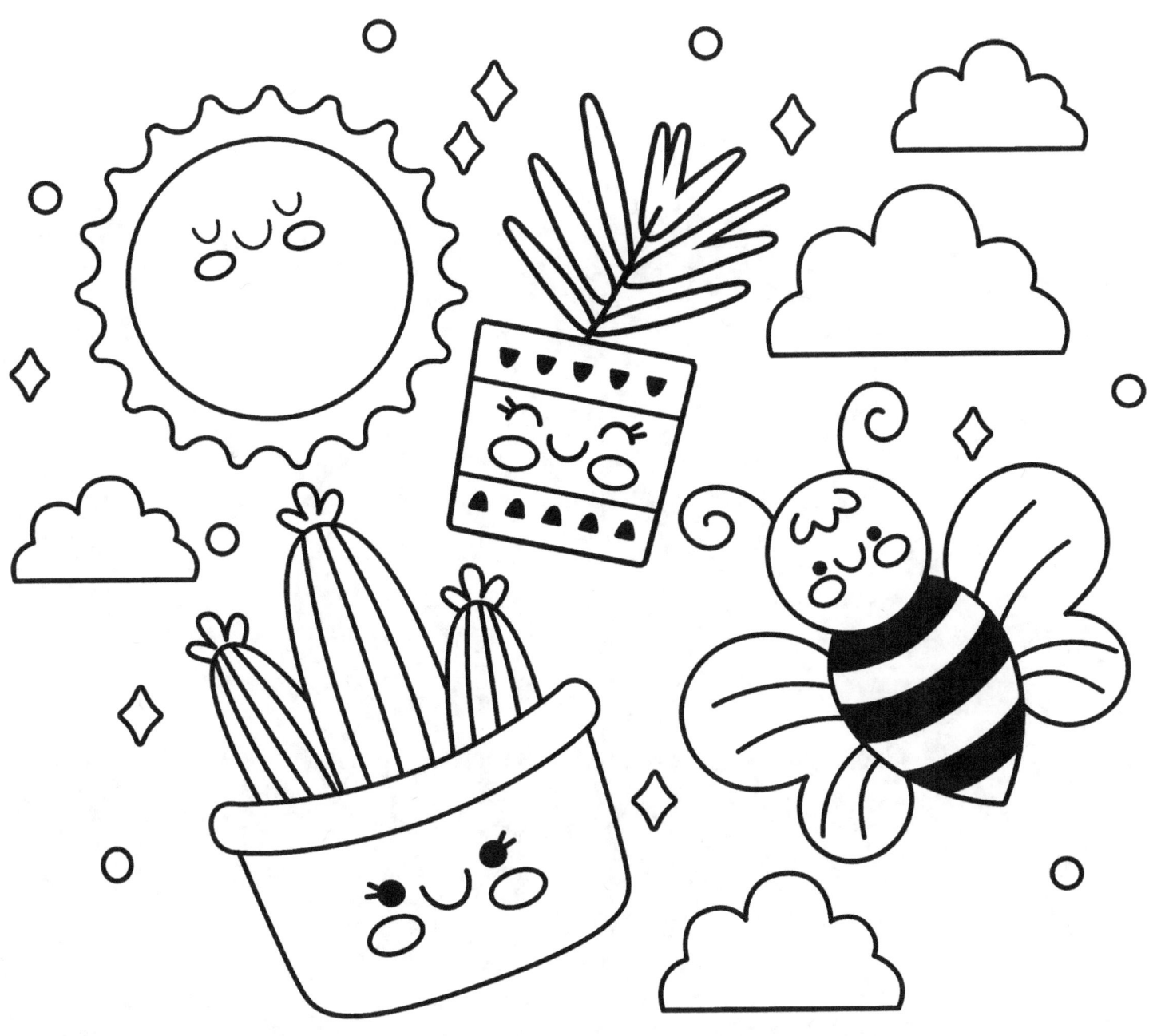

CUTE KAWAII
Coloring Book

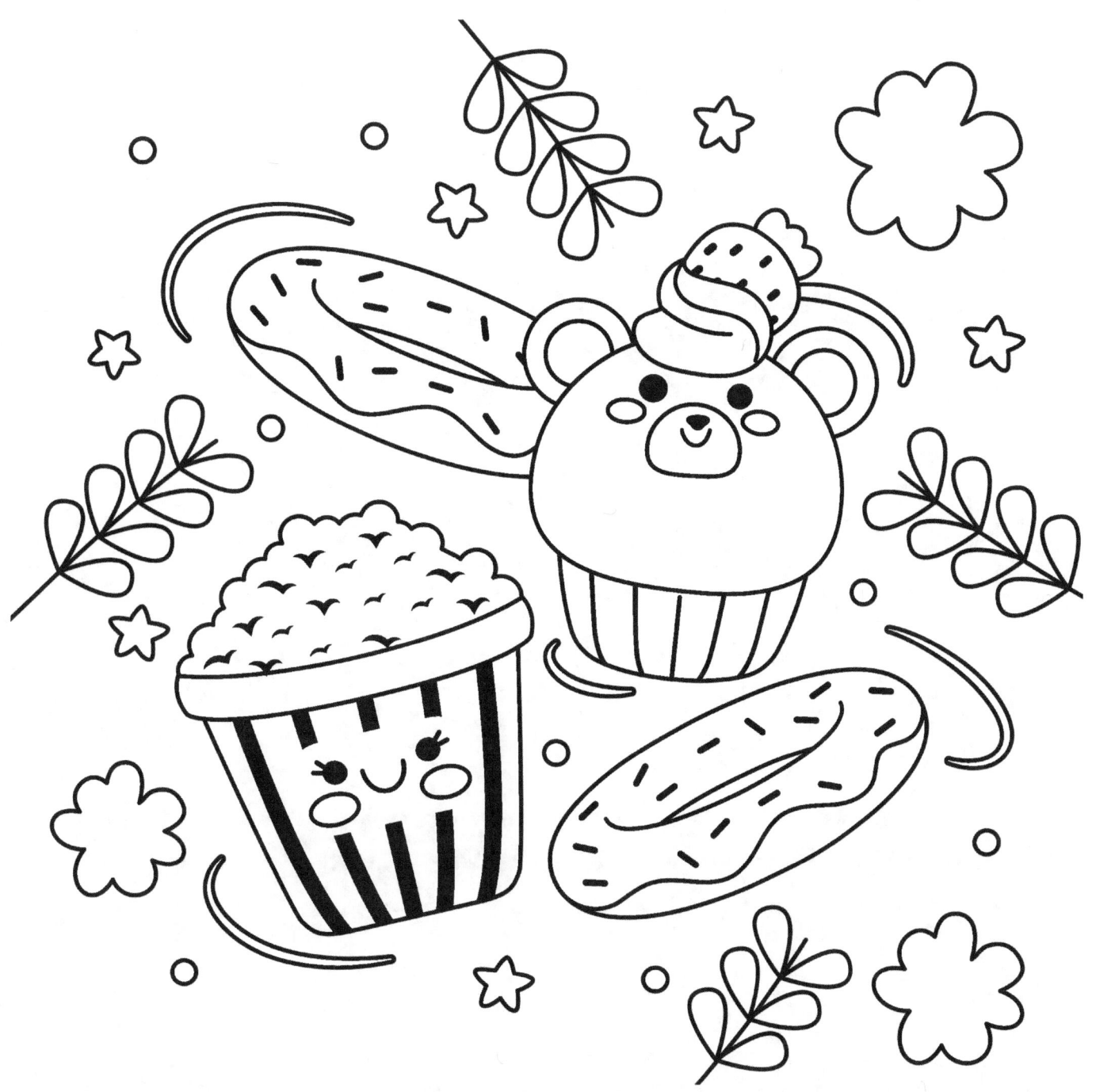

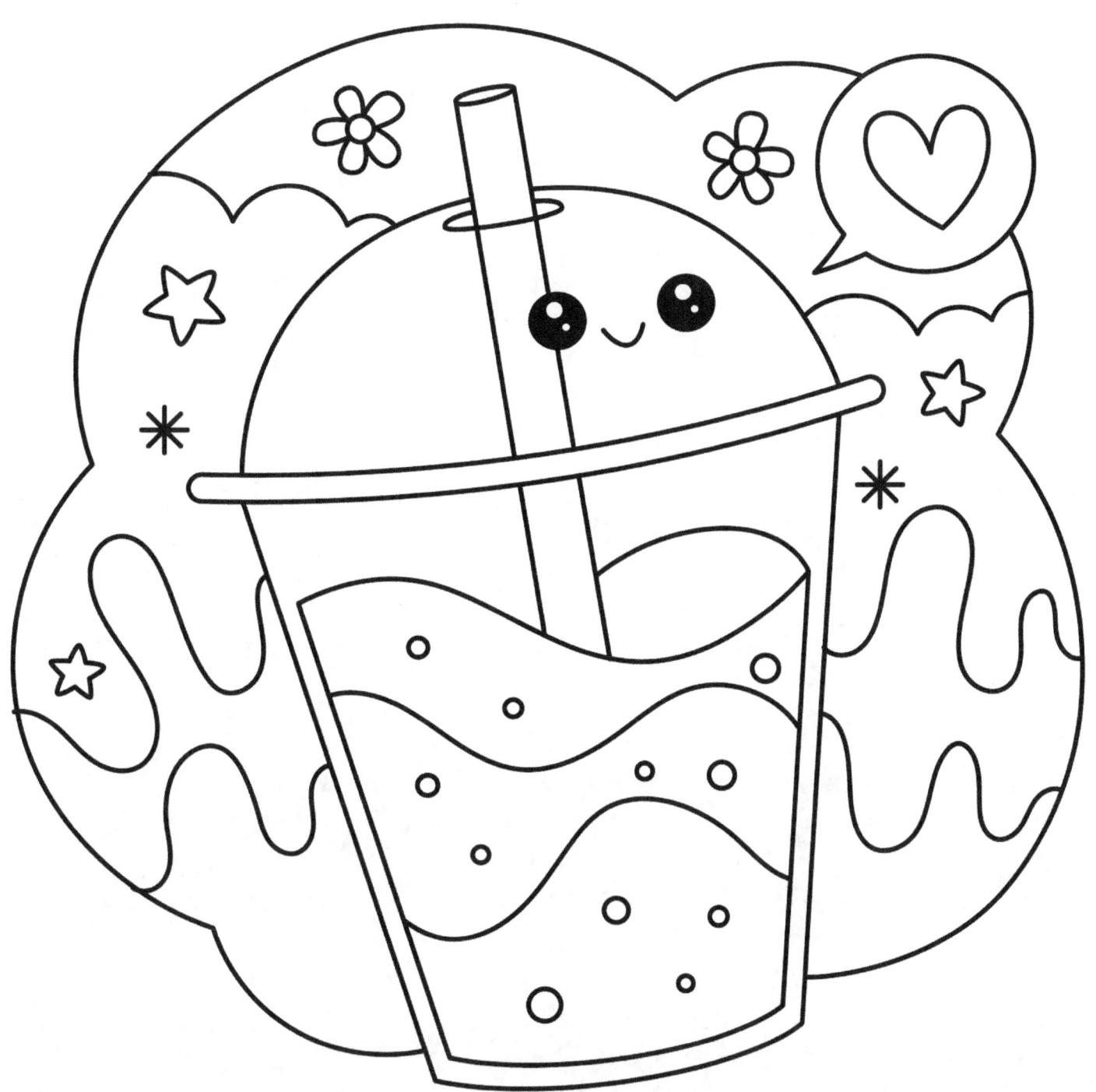

CUTE KAWAII
Coloring Book

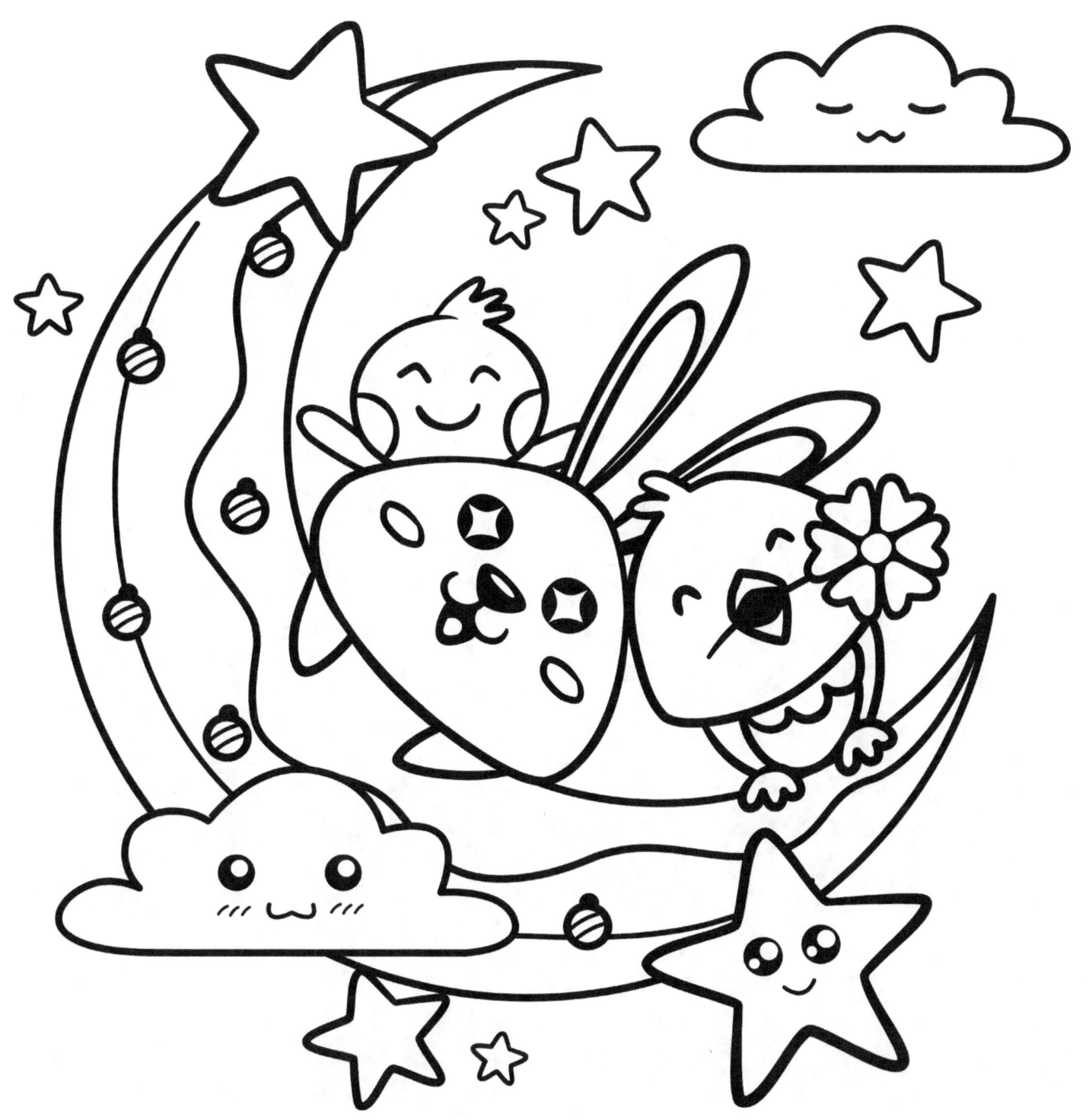

CUTE KAWAII
Coloring Book

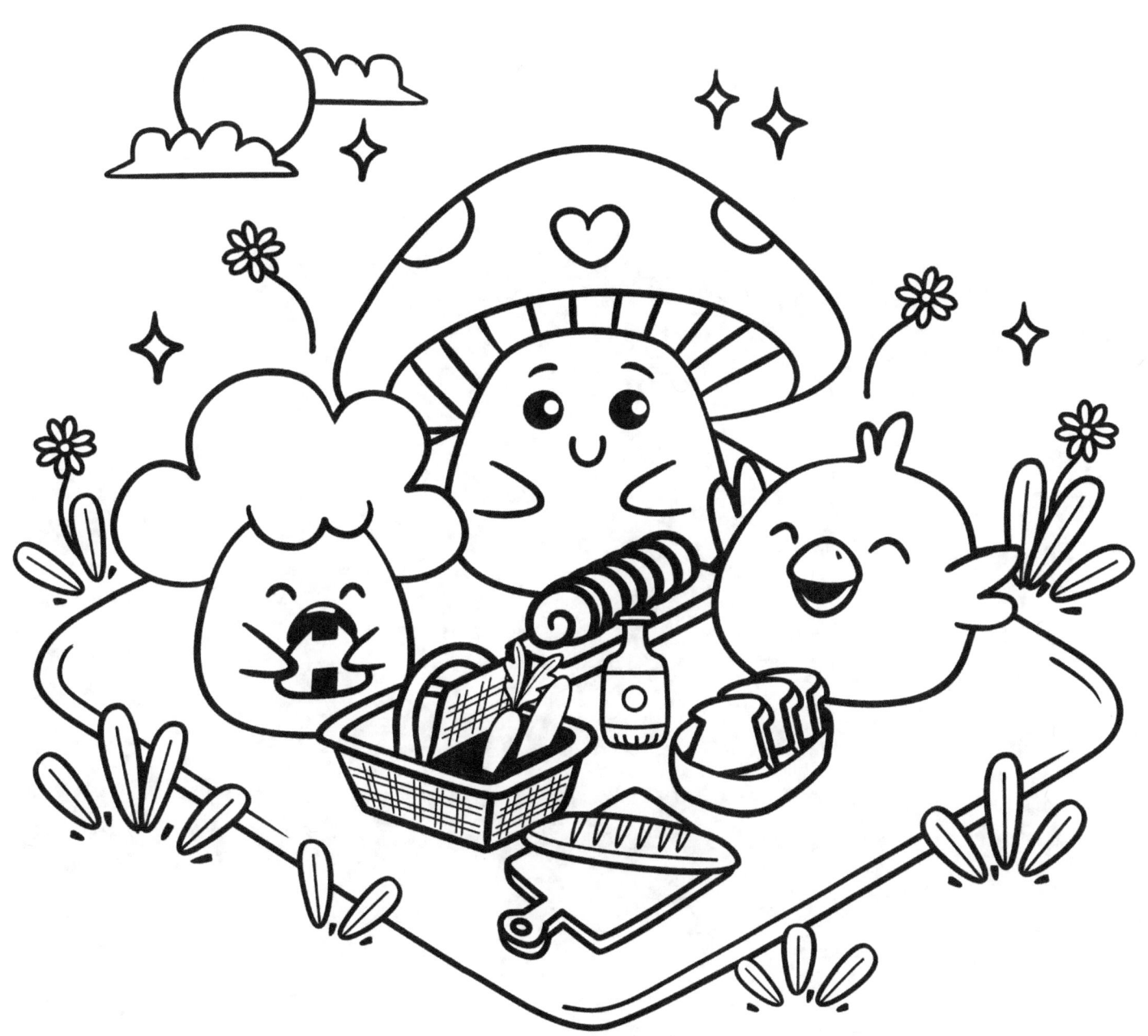